A Lionel
et Deborah

Bien Amicalement
Jacques
5/28/14

The Promise

The tale of two families betrayed by France and saved by the French

By Jacques Besnainou

Translated from the original French version by Johanna Sarriot

ISBN: 0991166302

ISBN-13: 978-0991166305

DEDICATION

To the love of my life, my wife Isabelle, who rescued me and gave me the courage to go on. To the lights of my life, my beloved children David, Sarah and Judith who are making me so proud every day.

CONTENTS

ACKNOWLEDGMENTS

This book would not have possible without all the members of my family who opened their minds and their hearts to retell this terrible story. A special thanks to my grand-aunt Zelma who gave me a very detailed account of the fate of the Holzer-Englander family, my wife's uncle Daniel, and my wife's father Albert who each gave a very detailed account of the fate of the Silberman family, including the precious postcards sent from the camps by Jeanne. Thank you also to the all the persons who reviewed and edited the book during the last year, in particular Veronique Warren-Guestault who edited the first French version, Johanna Sarriot who translated it, and Kersti Colombant and Rhonda Friedman who edited it the English translation. They provided me invaluable advice and ideas. Finally, I would like to recognize Nathalie Salmon and her husband, Bertrand Revert, who owns Comever - De Rameau publishing company in France. They supported my project from day one.

PROLOGUE

This book is the chronicle of a family's survival. The stories told in this tome stem from a promise I made to my mother, Renée Holzer-Englander-Besnainou, in 1977 when I was only 13 and she was losing her battle against breast cancer at the young age of 41.

She had invited me into her bedroom, in the back of our apartment on the Place de la Nation in Paris. For months now it had been clear to me that her health was deteriorating. She would lie down for long periods of time and had lost a great deal of weight. Her complexion grew paler by the day. I'd even come across the first draft of a letter she intended to write, telling me goodbye.

That night she made me promise two things: that I would continue to work diligently in school, for it was her belief that knowledge is the only asset a Jew can take with him wherever he goes; and that I would write a book telling the story of her family's sufferings and hardships during World War II.

Somehow, I had already understood the importance of the first promise; I had been working conscientiously at school to achieve straight As. The second promise, on the other hand, seemed far more problematic to fulfill. I didn't understand what could possibly have happened during the war that my mother would so desperately long for to the story be told. Up until that time, in my early adolescence, I hadn't even realized or thought about her involvement in the war. I later learned that my father had been outraged by her request and was deeply troubled that such a burden be placed on my young shoulders.

For ten years or so I put this promise on hold, concentrating instead on my studies and on starting a family with Isabelle, a wonderful young woman whom I met in college during my Freshman year. It was only in my late twenties, as I began a new life in the United States, that I developed an interest in the German Occupation of France. Like others interested in this topic, I had heard of the work of Robert Paxton, who was the first to bring to light the Vichy government's collaboration with the Nazis. I had read several books describing the horrors of the Vel' d'Hiv roundup and the abominable extermination of more than 4,000 Jewish children.

Then, in 1995, after President Jacques Chirac recognized the French government's active participation in the deportation of the Jews, my uncle Henri contacted me. He showed me the paperwork that he was filing to obtain reparations for the deportation of his father and the plundering of his personal goods during the war. Other family members began opening up to me as well. My mother-in-law, Gisèle, told me about her childhood experiences as a "hidden" child. Her brother, Michel, was also filing a demand for reparations for their suffering and for the deportation of their grandmother.

I decided that it was time to start gathering information. I had a red notebook and, from 1998 onward, began methodically interviewing every member of my own family, members of the Holzer family, and members of my wife's family, the Silbermans, who had also lived through the same time period. I discovered incredible stories of fear, hiding, brutality, fortune, and desperation. What's more, I was struck by the similarities between the two families in their struggle to survive during the war.

My mother's request was beginning to make sense. At a tender age, from four to eight years old, she had lived through a terrifying and inexplicable ordeal provoked by the willful blindness of a government gone mad. She had been rescued thanks to the miraculous intervention of simple and courageous people who had listened to their conscience and challenged the established order, often at the cost of their own lives. In 1940, about 330,000 Jews lived in France. Three-fourths of them survived thanks to the exemplary altruism of the French people. This book pays homage to them.

I know my mother would have wanted to write her own story, but a cruel disease took her at a young age. She was relying on me to carry this torch.

For a long time, my career was so pressing that I thought this book would have to wait until retirement. And then life, always full of surprises, presented me with a "sabbatical year." I took this gift of time to fulfill the promise. I worked from original documents sent by members of my family, along with online research and a wide variety of books. Every story and location, as well as most of the dates and names, are completely true albeit slightly romanticized in order to add texture and readability to this novelized history.

I hope that this book does more than fulfill a dying wish. I hope it serves to educate our children concerning a crime committed by purportedly "civilized" states so that such a thing never occurs again.

I take full responsibility for any inadvertent errors or omissions found in this book.

PART I - THE HOLZER- ENGLANDER FAMILY

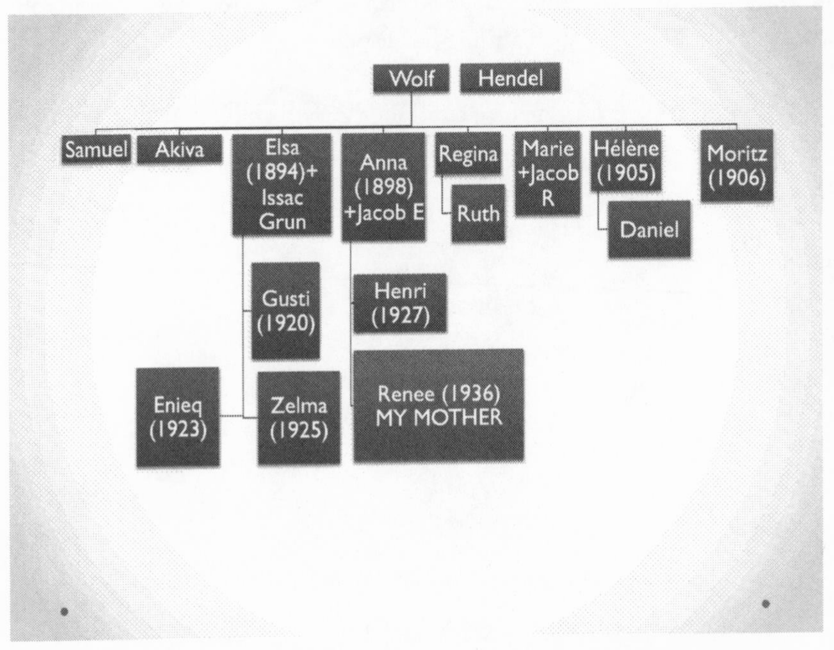

CHAPTER 1
1898
BORN IN KRYNICA
ANNA

Winter had shrouded the small village of Krynica in white, but spring was nearing and the mountains were finally turning green. The renowned hot springs in this southern region of Galicia started flowing again and, since the beginning of March, the light was slowly returning; the snow had melted into muddy slush, and spring flowers had raised their little heads. Life was emerging from its winter hibernation.

The village began preparing for its upcoming season of thermal baths as it did every year. In the spring of 1898, despite its altitude and its snowy slopes, Krynica was not the Polish ski resort that it has become today. Instead, it was recognized for its thermal springs. Every summer, the Polish bourgeoisie would travel to Krynica to rest and recuperate. Hotels and guesthouses that had been deserted during the winter were now booked solid from June to September.

The majority of the visitors were of Jewish origin, owners of thriving businesses that took them across Europe to Warsaw or Lodz. Krynica's warm sulfuric baths and its clean and invigorating air delighted these comfortably middle-class tourists. Under the clemency of Polish authorities, the Jewish bourgeoisie had prospered during the 19th century, dealing in commercial trades such as clothing, leather, jewelry and watch making. These nouveaux-riches were particularly fond of Galicia, and Krynica in particular thanks to its inns and hotels, which were often run by practicing Jewish families. This made it easier to observe strict kosher laws while still enjoying spa treatments and daily baths in the hot sulfuric springs of Krynica.

The Holzer family owned two of these hotels. Wolf, the father, had started his business about ten years earlier, borrowing money to buy his first guesthouse and devoting several years of especially hard work to launch and run the now thriving establishments.. His wife, Hendel, managed the kitchens with an iron fist, and the food was first-rate. She also had a flare for interior design and had decorated every room tastefully, though modestly.

On this particular evening of June 4, 1898, Hendel was not in the kitchen confirming that the vegetables being delivered were fresh, nor in the restaurant checking that the tables had been properly set. She wasn't even in the sitting room, where she often enjoyed listening to visitors' conversations while they relaxed after a day of intense massages and prolonged baths. Instead, Hendel was in their first floor apartment, covered in sweat and trying to hold her breath to keep from crying out. She was laboring to give birth to her fourth child.

Divine providence, or perhaps her own good nature, had already given her two rambunctious sons and a beautiful daughter. But today she worried that the labor was not progressing as it should. She felt it in her womb: though the baby was moving, something wasn't right. Doctor Hollander and the midwife, who had rushed to her side as soon as her water broke, were no longer smiling but concentrated instead on her lower belly.

Wolf was pacing in the entrance to the bedroom. Finally, between two contractions, Dr. Hollander exclaimed, "That's it! I can see the baby's bottom!" But why his bottom, wondered Hendel between moans of pain. Wasn't it usually the head that you saw first? That was it then; the baby was breech. Despite the fear running through her, she squeezed the midwife's hand and pushed with all her might.

And once again the miracle of life took place. The doctor took hold of the little bottom, then the shoulders, and finally the head of the baby, who made his appearance looking like a slimy blue ball and squirming in every direction. A good swat on the bottom and the baby suddenly turned red and howled out a first strident cry. " It's a girl! " announced the midwife. Hendel didn't hear her. The pain from that last push had made her faint.

But Wolf, who had heard the midwife's words, was already at his newborn daughter's side. Eyes filled with tears, he automatically counted her fingers and toes as generations of anxious Jewish fathers had done before him and always would. Wolf looked at her in wonder. Never mind the viscous bloody liquid that covered her. She was beautiful, despite the little cries and grimaces! He had almost forgotten Hendel, whom the doctor was currently fussing over to help her regain her spirits.

Finally, Hendel opened her eyes and, for the first time, saw her baby daughter lying in her husband's arms. He tenderly approached his wife and placed the baby, swaddled in clean white linen, into her arms. The tiny girl was no longer crying but purred softly as her eyes gazed around the room, seeking out the maternal gaze that she had not yet identified but could sense with her entire being. Wolf and Hendel were both moved. Though this wasn't their first child, the miracle of life still left them speechless. They barely had to consult each other before exclaiming, "Anna!" And so they named their new daughter.

Their happiness was complete. Wolf felt at home in Krynica. Though the Jewish community comprised only 15% of the 2,500 inhabitants of the spa resort, it was well integrated and respected. Wolf had worked hard with his wife to build their two guesthouses, and they were heavily indebted to Chaïm Cohen, their cousin in Warsaw. Business was good and Krynica was the ideal place to raise young children. The air was clean and there was plenty of room in the family apartment they called home, located on the second floor of one of their guesthouses.

On the night of June 4th, with the light still fading as they ate dinner, the Holzer household was brimming with joy. Hendel was recovering nicely. She sat at the table with Anna in her arms and her three other children, Samuel, Akiva, and Elsa, surrounding her. The rabbi was there, together with other leaders of the community, to celebrate Anna's birth with Wolf and Hendel.

Krynica was a safe haven for the Jews. There were no pogroms here; the Polish authorities were happy collecting the local taxes that resulted from the influx of tourists during the summer months. The government knew that the growth of tourism in this little community of southern Galicia was due in large part to the wealthy Jewish tourists who traveled from larger cities to rest and recuperate. There was, therefore, no question of detering visitors. In fact, the local police were careful to squelch any trace of anti-Semitism in the community.

There was a warm and cheerful atmosphere in the room that night. The rabbi made several toasts to the health of the Holzers and to little Anna, who wriggled in the arms of her mother. As the 19th century drew to a close, southern Galicia was a secure and lovely place for its Jewish families. They made plans for the future optimistically. Little did they know that the twentieth century would cast them into the depths of hell. That children, like Anna, would bear the full brunt of it, and very few would survive.

CHAPTER 2
1926
PASSOVER SEDER IN MANNHEIM
WOLF & HENDEL

The Holzer family in the 20's with Regina, Marie & Hélène in the front, Wolf & Hendel in the back (4th & 5th from the left)

The streets are crowded on this late afternoon. Moritz and his friend, Eran, struggle to push their way through the jostling throng. The Jewish quarter of Mannheim is a beehive of activity and teeming with people. Tonight is the first night of Pesach. For the past two days, fishermen, bakers, and butchers have been overwhelmed by demand. Everyone is bustling about, hurrying to prepare for this important evening with all its celebration. Moritz, about to turn twenty, is the baby of the Holzer family.

After Anna's birth came Regina, Marie, Hélène, and, finally, Moritz. Following her tenth pregnancy in 1906, Hendel and Wolf decided that the Lord had already blessed them with eight beautiful children (three boys and five girls survived) and that was enough. Business was good for Wolf, who had continued to prosper in Krynica until the start of the First World War.

It was then that Wolf quickly realized that Galicia, situated in the northeast of the Austro-Hungarian Empire, would be looked upon with greed by many, especially the rapacious Russians who, in Wolf's estimation, were anti-Semitic savages. It was even being reported that the Tsar's troops were frequently engaging in pogroms in villages that had large Israelite populations. The soldiers were notorious for raping and trafficking in young women. With five daughters, Wolf decided to sell his two hotels and find a safer place where he and Hendel could continue to raise their children under secure and happier circumstances.

At the time, there was no better destination than Germany. It had a remarkable policy of welcoming and integrating Jews, and the country would surely be the victor in this war, no matter how prolonged it was. But where would they go? It was Hendel who, in her great wisdom, found a solution. Why not rejoin Akiva, their second-born son, who was already in Mannheim studying at a yeshiva to perfect his knowledge of the Talmud?

The medium-sized city of Mannheim sat at the junction of the Rhine and Neckar Rivers. Hendel had found it charming when paying her son a visit in 1907. For one thing, it was incredibly easy to navigate. One of the only European cities to be organized along a grid, Mannheim's streets intersected at right angles. The city was divvied up into a series of squares of the same size. Each block could be identified by a number and a letter, just like a chessboard. Akiva's yeshiva, for instance, was located on the F2 block. Germans had even nicknamed the city "Quadratestadt," meaning the city of squares.

The Jewish community in Mannheim was powerful, prosperous, and well respected. Julius Dreyfuss was an influential member of the city council and a very important member of the community. Other Jews had become powerful and influential industrialists thanks to the precedent set by Victor Lenel. As the founder of the Rhine Rubber and Celluloid Factory and the vice-president of the Chamber of Commerce in Mannheim, he had become an example of the perfect integration of the Israelite community in Mannheim. Hendel convinced Wolf to consider settling down in this city in the south of Germany to protect their daughters from the Russian threat.

Wolf visited the city several times before finding the ideal property: a beautiful 18th century building on the H7 block, at number 13, which had four stories that formed a U-shape around a courtyard. The street entrance onto the courtyard was a magnificent porte-cochere made of sculpted wood. The walls were elegantly decorated, including carvings of delicate flowers along the second floor. It had high ceilings, perfectly maintained stairs, and flawless windowpanes. It was a perfect investment! They would rent out the twenty plus apartments and make the family home on the second floor of the building at the back of the courtyard, well removed from the noise of the city.

To sell his two hotels in Krynica, Wolf had been forced to negotiate with a Polish couple, who were exploiting the chaos created by the First World War. In the end, though, he managed to reach a satisfactory deal. Wolf had a large clientele that would guarantee continued revenue for the new owners, as long as they maintained the Holzer's standard of service. The next step was organizing the move to Mannheim. It hadn't been easy, particularly for Wolf, who understood that he was saying goodbye to some of his favorite activities, especially interacting with customers. But there was no choice as the Russians were closing in on Galicia and he couldn't afford to take a risk. Then again, in Mannheim he would finally have time to focus on his true passion – the study of the Torah and of philosophers such as Kant and Spinoza.

In 1917, the Holzer family began a new life in Germany and their adoptive city of Mannheim. The girls immediately felt at home. There was no language barrier; they had studied German from a young age. The city was an exciting place for teenagers compared to the small town of Krynica, where they were constantly bored, waiting for the cold nights of winter to end. Here in the city, they could walk to Planken Street, the main street in Mannheim, and sit on a café patio, listening to live music.

After the Great War ended in 1918, life returned to normal in Germany. The economy had been strangled by four years of armed conflict and a humiliating defeat, but it seemed to be slowly reviving. The apartments in the Holzer building were fairly easy to rent, leaving Wolf and Hendel free to focus on their children's education and on their daughters' matrimonial futures.

Anna's older sister, Elsa, was the first to marry. She introduced her parents to Isaac Grün, a boy from good, merchant stock in Mannheim. Their wedding was celebrated with great fanfare in Mannheim's principal synagogue. Soon after, the miracle of life once again took place as two adorable little girls were brought into the world – Gusti in 1920 and Zelma in 1925 – to the delight of their grandparents.

In 1923, Anna was 25 years old and had never brought home a suitor. Hendel worried about Anna's prospects. Although Anna had interest in men and was beautiful, little Anna (for she was small in stature) had a strong personality. Blessed with a keen intelligence, she was not impressed easily. Anna had high expectations for a marriage; her husband would have to be talented, competent, capable, of great stature and, above all, hard working. Most of the young men in Mannheim that she met at Synagogue or in cafés did not interest her. Born into wealthy families, many of these youths were cocky and far too pleased with themselves. They were more inclined to drink and party at night than devote themselves to a career.

Moritz and Eran, both panting from exertion, finally arrive at the carriage entrance of the Holzer building. Hendel spots them from the kitchen window and shouts, "There you are, Moritz! Your father is looking everywhere for you. Hurry up! We're about to start the prayer." Moritz and Eran barely have time to catch their breaths before being ushered into the large living room where the entire family was assembled.

As family patriarch, Wolf is already seated at the head of the table. He has been reviewing the text from the Haggadah, which will help him lead the prayers and ensure that the ingredients for the ritual are arranged correctly on the table. The matza is there, of course. A piece of matza has even been hidden under the tablecloth for the children to find. The most important item on the table, however, is the lamb shoulder bone, which symbolizes the power of God when he freed the Israelite slaves from Pharaoh. It is surrounded by bitter herbs that symbolize the bitter years of slavery in Egypt, a boiled egg that represents life, and "charoset," a strange blend of fruits and nuts that recalls the mortar and adobe bricks the Israelites made in ancient Egypt.

"Ah! There you are, Moritz. We're all waiting for you. You and Eran, go wash your hands, and then take a seat next to me. We're about to start the prayer," said Wolf in a firm but pleasant voice. Everyone takes a place around the table. The ceremony is about to begin.

CHAPTER 3
1933
A HORRIFYING PARADE IN MANNHEIM
ZELMA

Elsa's daughter, Zelma is now a smart and vivacious eight-year-old girl. What she is about to experience on this lovely spring day will forever be branded in her memory as a day of appalling terror – the day when her entire life changed and her innocence was lost forever.

It is a sunny day in April and Zelma is running excitedly alongside her mother to watch the parade in the center of town. They arrive at Planken Street, spot the soldiers marching by, and understand immediately that this is a turning point – their lives are about to be derailed.

The soldiers' boots thump along the pavement, their chants loud and haunting. The words spewing from their mouths make no sense: "May the blood of the Jews flow from our knives!" And then, the most appalling sight of all: a cart rolling by with an old man locked in a cage; a sign marked "Jew" hanging from his neck.

Zelma is terrified. She presses herself closer against her mother, who is sobbing quietly. They both want to leave but are trapped by the crowd that applauds and cheers, their right arms stiffened and raised in pride. Zelma doesn't understand. How could her friendly neighbors be cheering on these savages who would cage an old man like an animal and call for the death of Jews? The people around her seem to be celebrating this parade of men. So many colors and flags! So much excitement! The soldiers' boots hit the pavement in noisy unison. Their uniforms are jet black. Power and brute strength emanate from the SS as they march by.

Elsa and Zelma are finally able to leave. The fearsome troops have passed and the onlookers are dispersing. Elsa keeps a firm grip on Zelma's hand and heads toward their home on H7 Street as quickly as possible, keeping close to the walls. Everything has changed in an instant. This cosmopolitan city, once so welcoming and hospitable, now seems gray, austere, and full of hateful, evil people. Zelma's entire body is trembling – she had felt as though she would be trampled to death when the brutal horde had paraded past. The ominous marching and chanting echoes on in her mind.

They finally reach their home and head straight for their grandfather's apartment. Wolf is doing his usual morning reading. Elsa, and Zelma in particular, tell him what they saw. He ponders in silence for a moment then rises from his chair and says, "We are about to go through a very difficult period – not only us, but a large part of the world, and Judaism as a whole. I believe we are headed for another world war." Wolf is familiar with Hitler's main book *Mein Kampf* ("My Struggle") and understands the situation well. He places a hand on Elsa and Zelma's heads and blesses them. "It's going to be all right. You must be brave!"

He then tells them the story of Rabbi Jochanan Ben Sakai. "During the reign of Titus, when the Romans had destroyed the Second Temple and set fire to Jerusalem, the rabbi gathered his pupils around him. He asked them to smuggle him out of the city in a coffin and to take him to Javneh where he could establish a new yeshiva. The students asked, 'What does it matter? All is lost!' But the rabbi replied, 'No! Even scattered in a diaspora, a people will continue to thrive so long as its culture and its knowledge remain.'"

That night, the entire family gathers around the table. Grandfather Wolf is the first to speak. "My children, we are about to embark on difficult times, and I understand if some of you wish to leave Germany in the wake of this madness. But I am too old, and I was already forced to leave my home once before, in Galicia. I'm not going anywhere." The faces around the table look sad and defeated.

Then, one by one, the men in the family speak up. Akiva explains that, as his studies at the yeshiva are now finished, he wishes to return to Poland to join his brother Samuel who runs a prosperous business in Krakow. "They may be anti-Semitic over there, but they haven't gone mad like the Nazis."

Elsa's husband, Isaac Grün, prefers to keep his family in Mannheim for the moment. He was born and raised in this city and believes that this folly will eventually pass. Besides, the Jews are powerful here; what could possibly happen to them?

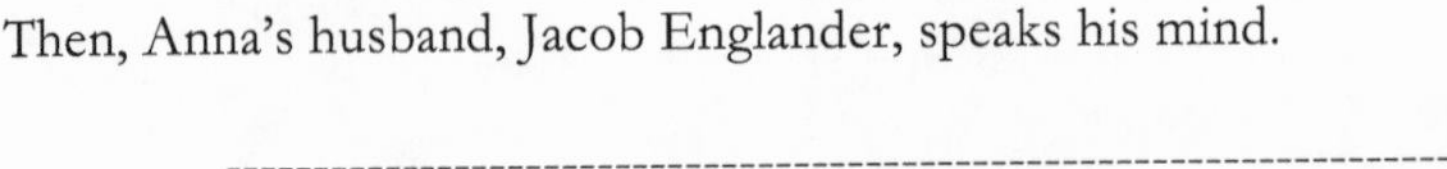

Then, Anna's husband, Jacob Englander, speaks his mind.

Anna and Jacob Englander were wed in 1926. They met, by chance, in the main square of Mannheim. Anna immediately took a liking to Jacob. He was a large man and was born in Galicia, just like her, in 1893. He was a certified watchmaker – a skill that had been passed down from father to son in the Englander family. In 1916, when he was twenty-three years old, Jacob's life took an unexpected turn. He was drafted into the Austrian army and dispatched to the Russian front. When he returned from the war, he was profoundly affected by the horrors he had seen. He developed a loathing for Bolsheviks and a reticence toward weapons and the military in general.

He settled down in Frankfurt with his father and met Anna while visiting Mannheim on business. They immediately hit it off, despite their notorious height difference – Anna was barely five feet tall to Jacob's six foot two. She loved his serious side and his maturity. He loved her vivacious spirit and her strength of character. Hendel was delighted that her daughter had finally found a husband! She was even more elated when little Henri was born in 1927 from this union.

Jacob has no faith in the Jews' ability to stand up to the brutal folly of the Nazis. He prefers to leave and perhaps go to Paris, where he hopes to open a small watch repair shop. Apparently, watchmakers were in demand in Paris. And besides, "France won the Great War; the Nazis wouldn't dare come up against them again." His son, Henri, is only six years old, the perfect age for learning a new language, starting afresh, and adopting a new country. It may be even good for Jacob to travel and learn a new language.

Finally it is Moritz's turn, the youngest of the Holzer siblings, to speak up. At twenty-seven years old, he has little to tie him down in Mannheim. For the past seven years he has worked as an apprentice, specializing in tapestries at the Weiss shop. But he has yet to find a wife and is bored by this medium-sized town in Germany. He craves adventure and dreams of traveling beyond the Atlantic Ocean. This is the perfect opportunity for him, and he decides to buy a ticket for America as soon as possible.

Wolf has been sitting quietly and listening. "My children, I give you my blessing, and I will support each of your decisions. Though we may be separated for a few years, I hope that we can visit each other often, and I pray we are reunited once Hitler is gone. His thoughts return to Rabbi Ben Sakai's words over and over again: "Even scattered in a diaspora, a people will continue to thrive so long as its culture and its knowledge remain."

That night, supper is finished in silence. It has been an intense day and the Holzer family, though together for the moment, knows that it will soon be separated.

CHAPTER 4
1936
REBIRTH IN PARIS
JACOB

Anna and baby Renée, 1936

Renée and Henri, 1937

It's a beautiful day. Under a clear blue sky, an air of festivity has descended on the city of lights. Tricolor flags flutter in the wind over one of the most majestic public spaces in the world, the Esplanade des Invalides. Jacob has brought his family here to cheer on the soldiers of the French Republic, for they represent the best defense against the Nazis.

Jacob is pleased. He made the right choice in moving his family to the French capital three years ago, though the adjustment was harder than expected.

Starting over in France had been tough and problematic. Jacob, Anna, and Henri first lived in a decrepit old hotel in the 3rd arrondissement. The room smelled of mold and failed to keep out the winter cold, which quickly seeped into their bones. It had been difficult to find work during the first few weeks, as Jacob's papers were not in order. Fortunately, just as he had anticipated, his skills as a watchmaker were very much in demand.

After stopping by every shop in the Jewish quarter, he was finally hired by a man named Moshe Ziegler, who recognized the value of Jacob's nimble fingers. He could fix any watch or clock in record time. Huddled over his stool at the back of the shop, armed with a loupe and a small screwdriver, Jacob could methodically dismantle even the most complex of mechanisms. He would line up the tiny parts and springs on a piece of soft felt in front of him, in an order that only he understood. Then, using a tiny brush, he would carefully clean the watchcase, reaching deep into its corners before lubricating the gears with a few drops of oil and checking for the proper tension of the springs.

His favorite step was rewinding the mechanism precisely and adeptly when he was finished. It was like a game for him, a puzzle that only he could unravel. His boss, Moshe, would time him just so he could tell his clients that Ziegler's held the fastest record for winding watches.

Times were extremely hard in 1934 and 1935, but the stability of being a watchmaker was a lifesaver and kept the family afloat in their new life in Paris. The succession of governments in France following the depression were often anti-Semitic or, at best, anti-German. Jacob had two strikes against him: he was both Jewish and German. These traits became immediately apparent as soon as spoke and, on several occasions, landed him in the police station. He had even served a few weeks' time in a detestable prison with other common law detainees in Fresnes, a suburb south of the city. Moshe Ziegler had paid his bail thanks to his connections in the upper echelons of the police department. He needed his best worker back at the shop, and that was Jacob!

Moshe had also helped Jacob find permanent lodging by serving as the guarantor for a small line of credit that allowed the family to purchase an apartment at 62 rue de Saintonge, located in the 3rd arrondissement, a district near the Place de la République. The apartment was barely 430 square feet but included a bedroom, a living room, and a very tiny kitchen. Anna and Jacob immediately felt at home there. Most of their neighbors – with whom they shared a "Turkish toilet" on the landing between floors – were also Jewish, hardworking families with the same desire to give their children a chance at a better life, away from the Nazis, under the protection of the French Republic. And though the building was a bit run down – the stairs were worn from use and the dining room floor was slanted – there was a warmth and a sense of community that put Jacob and his family immediately at ease.

After several months, Anna succeeded in purchasing a Singer sewing machine. Made of black Bakelite and trimmed with gold filigree, this magical device enabled her to sew at a fast pace, thanks to its ingenious pedal mechanism. She immediately set about creating a lovely pair of curtains for her bedroom, earning the admiration of her neighbors. Anna had pluck, and she had talent. Word of mouth spread quickly, and before long she had been commissioned to make curtains for her next-door neighbor, Esther. Soon Esther's sister, Sarah, was also ordering curtains from Anna. In a matter of just a few months, Anna had steady business coming in on a daily basis. She spent her afternoons working at her darling sewing machine, next to the open window where she could feel the breeze from the courtyard, smell the meals that were being prepared, and hear the children who played ball outside. Life was indeed delightful in the country of Voltaire. It appeared the old Yiddish saying, "Wie Gott in Frankreich," was true. You could live like a god in France!

Thanks to Moshe's clout within the police department, strings were pulled again and Jacob eventually obtained political refugee status for himself, Anna, and Henri. In September 1934, he was able to enroll Henri in a primary school on the rue Béranger, not two hundred meters from their apartment. Although Henri already spoke excellent French and was seven years old, the principal placed him in the first grade, wanting to be sure he developed a solid foundation in the written language. Henri proved to be a brilliant student, however, and surprised everyone with how quickly he learned to read and write. His first grade teacher, Mrs. Garnier, immediately recognized his abilities and, within a few months, moved him up to the second grade with children his own age. Jacob was astounded by his son's lightning-quick progress. By June 1935, Henri spoke French fluently, with a perfect accent, and could even read the newspaper. He would sit on Jacob's lap every evening, rapidly deciphering and translating the main articles in the French newspaper *l'Humanité* for his father. Jacob greatly enjoyed following current events closely in France, especially the struggle against fascism. He had tremendous admiration for Léon Blum, a rising French politician who was also Jewish. Blum wrote incendiary articles condemning the French right and the extreme right, and was barraged with anti-Semitic articles in return.

Jacob sensed that an insidious change was taking place in France. On February 6, 1934, a series of bloody riots had exposed the undercurrents of violence and fascism that ran amongst the right and the extreme right. Léon Blum had teamed up with Maurice Thorez, a communist politician who was also a prolific contributor to *l'Humanité*, in an effort to keep France from following the fascist example of Germany or Italy. It was through Henri's assiduous daily reading that Anna and Jacob witnessed the birth of the Popular Front and the historic elections of May 1936.

Morale was high for Anna and Jacob, who were blessed on February 25, 1936 with the birth of a baby girl. In their enthusiasm, they chose to give her a French name, Renée, which means "reborn" in French, in honor of their rebirth in Paris. Jacob loved his newborn daughter, with her large blue-green eyes and blonde head of fine baby's hair.

Henri was proud of his new baby sister and would stare at her for hours on end as she squirmed around happily in her crib. Like his parents, he took great joy in this new addition to the family. He had waited a long time for a sibling and had often asked Jacob and Anna for a baby brother or sister to ease the solitude of being an only child. Though he had seen his mother's stomach grow bigger over the fall, at eight years old he could not truly fathom how such an adorable creature had come into the world. As they were reading together one evening, Jacob explained to his son that he had planted a seed in his mother's tummy that would grow into a little brother or sister. The explanation, though vague, seemed to satisfy Henri who now took great pleasure in watching each new accomplishment as Renée grew and developed. He especially loved the radiant smile that broke across her face every time she spotted him.

Today, Jacob is euphoric! Renée is in her stroller making spit bubbles, Henri is wriggling with impatience, and Anna is standing closely by his side. They arrive early and stake out a spot right up against the rope line, waiting for the magical 14th of July parade to start. Off in the distance, the palatial golden dome of the Hôtel des Invalides glistens in the dazzling sunlight. The crowd grows larger and more excited by the second. The Blum government has declared a three-day holiday party in honor of the people, the military, and France.

Finally! The parade is about to start! The first to go by are infantrymen whose footsteps resound as they head toward the ornate Alexander III Bridge; they are led by the engineering students of the prestigious Polytechnic military school, all decked out in black with strangely-shaped bicorn hats placed tightly on top of their heads. Next are the cadets from the special military school of Saint-Cyr, in magnificent red uniform trousers and their funny, feathered hats. Jacob and his family are most excited by the cavalrymen who come next. How splendid, how imposing the Republican Guard is! They prance by in perfect cadence, heads held high under their golden helmets with the famous red-feathered plume proudly erect. Naturally, all of this pageantry is accompanied by the steady rhythm of military music sweeping majestically over the entire procession.

Suddenly, the armored vehicles appear – odd-looking machines, rolling along on caterpillar tracks with a deafening noise. These are the new battle tanks of the French army, which were promoted by a certain Lieutenant Colonel by the name of Charles de Gaulle. Jacob is familiar with the vehicles. Henri read him a long article on the new armored and motorized regiments that were guaranteed to defend France against any possible attack.

Jacob is so happy! He made the right choice. France has finally proven itself hospitable, powerful and invincible. Here he can confidently watch Renée and Henri grow up in peace and tranquility.

CHAPTER 5
1940
BROÛT-VERNET
HENRI

The door opens and there's Papa! After so many months of anguish and separation, there he is – in his beautiful Sunday suit, with his neat round glasses, and a pencil mustache framing his signature grand smile! Henri's happiness knows no bounds. He throws himself into his father's arms. Finally! He came! Henri still can't believe it.

When Principal Bass, a tall, imposing figure with white hair, came to find him at recess to walk him to her office, he had wondered what more could possibly befall him in addition to these terrible months of separation. He had instructed his sister, Renée, to keep playing nicely with her friends. And then, to his great surprise, the principal had opened the door to her office to reveal his father, face alight with that amazing bright smile! The long weeks of waiting with no news were over at last; Jacob had finally come to collect Henri and his little sister.

Everything had unraveled in June. Jacob had promised that the French army could protect them against the Nazis. For once, he was wrong.

Beginning in May, the war of position – or Phony War as the newspapers were calling it – had turned into a mechanized, lightning strike war that had quickly defeated the French troops. Henri noticed his father's increasing worry when they read the newspaper at night. Government propaganda swore that the magic of the "Battle of the Marne of 1914" would repeat itself and the German hordes would be thwarted by the cunning and courage of the French armies. But Henri and his parents understood that the situation was worsening day by day and that the dreaded Nazis were closing in on the capital.

Jacob's suspicions were confirmed when German bombing of the capital city intensified at the beginning of June. He knew then that they had to leave, if only for a short while, to put the greatest distance possible between them and the advancing German troops. They would head for the south of France. Only a few weeks earlier, Anna's sister, Elsa, had been forced to leave her new home in Belgium to escape the Nazi onslaught. In 1938, Elsa and her husband Isaac had finally decided to leave Mannheim for Brussels after the situation in Germany became unbearable. Now, in 1940, her family had to flee again and landed in Revel, a small French town in the southwestern region of Haute Garonne, near Toulouse. Jacob and Anna decided to join them, at least for a little while.

Jacob turned to his old boss, Moshe Ziegler, for advice. In September 1936, Jacob had successfully opened his own watch shop in the northern Parisian suburb of St-Denis. Moshe had lived in France for much longer than Jacob and could not imagine the French army being defeated. But he could understand Jacob's anguish, particularly after listening to his detailed stories of the Nazi savagery that had flared up so suddenly in Mannheim. Moshe promised to watch over Jacob's shop in St-Denis for the few weeks that he would be away.

Anna carefully prepared for their departure and tidied up their little apartment on the rue de Saintonge. She left a second set of house keys with her neighbor, Esther, and warned her of their imminent departure. Finally, on Sunday, June 5, Anna, Jacob, and their two children, taking only three suitcases packed with the bare essentials, left their little apartment to board a train at the Austerlitz station. They were leaving a few days earlier than planned, for the situation was escalating faster than anticipated. Official communication from the French government had become increasingly incoherent and Jacob understood, reading between the lines, that the government was actually withdrawing to Bordeaux. The sirens that usually signified nocturnal bombings had started blaring incessantly and the resulting damage was more and more apparent. Anna had been particularly shocked to see that the front of a famous café, facing the Place de la République, had been completely destroyed. The enemy was getting closer. The final proof was the ever-increasing number of refugees flooding into Paris; their dazed and terrified faces bespoke the horrors they were fleeing and which were now fast approaching Paris.

Pandemonium reigned in the Austerlitz station that day. Thousands of people had slept among the litter on the bare floor. Women were yelling, children crying, and the police were visibly struggling to control the crowd. Jacob's conclusions were obviously accurate. Wild rumors were running rampant; the train on which he had reservations was flagged as one of the very last authorized to leave the capital and head south. The armed conflict was nearing, making train travel increasingly dangerous. A crazed mob had gathered and was pressed up against the security barrier that blocked access to the platform. Everyone was trying desperately to get on board what was rumored to be the "last" train.

Henri thought they couldn't possibly make it to the coveted train cars, but his father's great height saved them. With Renée held tightly in his arms, Jacob cut a path through the crowd, yelling that he did have tickets for this train! Anna and Henri stayed glued to his tracks, following closely on his heels. The policeman blocking the entrance to the platform had spotted the tall fellow with a pronounced German accent who seemed determined to get through. He asked for the family's papers and train tickets. After determining that the Englander family did, in fact, have the right to board the train, he opened the barrier and let Jacob, Henri, Anna, and Renée through, with their three suitcases in tow.

They found their compartment easily and immediately collapsed into their seats, astounded that they had made it through the mad crush of people.

The train finally pulled out of the station, a good two hours late, leaving a trail of white steam in its wake as it began its long trek toward the south of France. It was packed with people. Aside from the usual passengers sitting in their rightful compartments, the hallways were crammed every which way with those who had apparently managed to persuade either the policemen or the conductor that they absolutely needed to be on board that train!

The sight of all this desperation only reinforced Jacob's conviction that they needed to get as far away from the German invasion as possible. The mad rush that he had just witnessed, along with what Henri had read to him from the latest edition of *l'Humanité*, had destroyed any remaining faith he had in the great army of the French Republic. The Englanders had to put the greatest distance possible between themselves and Germany!

When the conductor finally managed to create a path to the family's compartment, Henri was the one to show him their tickets to Toulouse and to ask about the quickest method to Revel from there. His French was perfect, unlike his parents'. The conductor responded, "Getting to Revel is quite simple. A shuttle train leaves from Toulouse twice a day." Jacob decided immediately to pay the extra fare that would get them from Toulouse to Revel. And that is how, on the morning of June 6, 1940, Henri, Anna, Jacob, and Renée came to find themselves in a little town in the foothills of the Pyrénées Mountains, after more than sixteen hours of grueling travel.

Here they would be far removed from the frenetic bustle of Paris. On this lovely morning in June, the town seemed peaceful, warm, and welcoming, almost as if it were asleep. It felt perfectly natural for them to settle into a little room at the station hotel.

The following days were dedicated to exploring the region, reuniting with the rest of their family, and devising a plan of action for the weeks ahead. Jacob's worst fear had been confirmed: the French army had surrendered. Toward the end of June, the capitulation was finalized and France was divided into an occupied zone and a free zone. Jacob and Anna understood then that they would not be returning to Paris any time soon. They needed to accept the fact that they might be staying for several months, or even years, in this new region. However, Jacob only had a few months' worth of savings with him. He would need to find a job soon. They also needed to find better accommodations than the small hotel room that they had all shared since their arrival in Revel.

Fortunately, Elsa had found an ideal place to live thanks to a retired carpenter renting his old workshop. Jacob, Anna, and their children settled into the spacious quarters with Elsa and her husband, and their daughter Zelma, who was only two years older than Henri, Anna's baby sister, Hélène, and her third sister, Regina, along with Regina's daughter Ruth. Four Holzer sisters were now living under the same roof and, despite the precarious nature of the situation, they were delighted by this unexpected reunion.

It was Anna who thought of taking the children to Broût-Vernet, near Vichy, where Marshal Pétain's newly formed government was located. Anna had heard about the OSE from her Jewish neighbors on the rue de Saintonge and the boulevard du Temple. The OSE, a children's aid society, that offered assistance to Jewish families in need, had opened a center for children in a small chateau nicknamed the Morelles House.

On a sunny morning in July 1940, Anna and Jacob arrived at the imposing white building in Broût-Vernet and entrusted their two small children, Henri and Renée, to Ms. Alexandra Bass.

It was Renée's first time being separated from her parents and she burst into tears upon realizing that Jacob and Anna were leaving her there, in the hands of strangers. Fortunately, Henri was staying with her and would not leave her side. Anna and Jacob had instructed him to look after her. "We're counting on you. You're almost thirteen years old, already a man in the eyes of the Jewish faith. You must watch over Renée like she was the apple of your eye."

Henri took his parents' words to heart. After they left, he hugged Renée tight until her sobs subsided and her fears were calmed.

Life at the Morelles House was not unpleasant. Ms. Bass was a doctor, originally from Russia. Despite her stiff exterior, she had a huge heart. Vaccinations were required for all children, so Henri and Renée were subjected to the fearful syringes as soon as they arrived. Their religious education was provided at the Morelles House and Henri applied himself faithfully to preparing for his upcoming bar mitzvah. Their secular education occured at the Broût-Vernet primary school that the children attended, accompanied each day by counselors from the Morelles House.

Henri became friends with a young girl his age named Léa Katz, who was also responsible for her two little brothers, one five and the other six-and-a-half-years old. Like two shipwrecked survivors, Henri and Léa looked out for each other and shared in each other's joys and sorrows as they struggled with the uncertainty of their future and the separation from their parents.

Time seemed to go slowly for Henri, who hadn't heard from his parents since July. A first postcard arrived in September, then another in October. Anna explained that Jacob was close to finding work. His skills as a watchmaker, along with the glowing recommendation that his previous employer, Moshe, had written him, would surely open many doors. Henri wasn't sure how much to believe, however, and was beginning to worry.

Today, all of Henri's concerns are put to rest. Jacob is standing squarely in front of him, explaining to Miss Bass that he has come to take Henri and Renée home. He has finally found steady work at the Bonnefont boutique in Castelnaudary, a little town located 20 km from Revel in south west of France, and already rented a little house there for the family at number 29 rue de la Comédie.

Henri's joy knows no bounds! With Ms. Bass's permission, he rushes off to find Renée who is playing hopscotch in the courtyard. Henri pulls eagerly on his little sister's sleeve and the two run toward their father who is just a few paces behind. At the sight of Jacob's tall figure and the beloved sound of his low voice addressing her in German, Renée leaps into her father's arms. He picks her up in one sweeping motion and swings her high above his head before covering his little girl's cheeks with kisses.

Henri weeps with joy. His father is proud of him for faithfully keeping his promise and protecting his little sister as "the apple of his eye." Their long separation is finally over. Now they can build a new life in Castelnaudary.

CHAPTER 6
1943
THE TANAKH IN THE CHURCH
FATHER PUECH

Sunlight filters through the colorful stained-glass windows and caresses the walls of the church on this late afternoon in December. Father Puech, the director of the Castres Minor Seminary – also known as the Barral School – sits at his desk, with Henri at his side. They meet two Thursdays every month, away from prying eyes, in late afternoon, to study a chapter of the Tanakh – in the original Hebrew. Today's topic is Abraham's sacrifice. Together they run their fingers over the ancient Hebrew text as Abraham, the great centenarian, comes to life before them. They see his tortured struggle as the Lord asks him for the ultimate sacrifice of his only son, Isaac. They follow his heavy but determined steps up Mount Moriah. Father Puech leads Henri through the scripture reading, using Abraham and Isaac's story to demonstrate the profound resilience of the human spirit. They reflect for a long time upon young Isaac's question, "Where is the sacrificial lamb?" and his father's response, "The Lord will provide it."

Father Puech is now thirty-seven years old. He is an experienced priest – deeply pious and erudite. He was born in the southwest of France, in the department of the Tarn and, after studying at the Barral School, was ordained in 1930. The priest felt his calling was in education, so it seemed only natural to begin teaching at the school where he himself had been educated.

The Barral School is a beautiful white building with a large wooden cross adorning its magnificent frontispiece. Nestled in a bend of the Tarn River, to the south of Castres, in the southwest of France, the school is open to boys from sixth grade onward; its goal is to provide a Catholic education, while fostering a vocation for the priesthood.

Father Puech, the director of the Barral School since July 1940, has a tolerant approach to teaching Catholicism. Although the primary function of the school is to provide a religious education and encourage priestly vocations, the abbot strongly believes that such vocations cannot be forced upon an individual. His role is not to select new priests but to provide counsel to these young souls and enlighten them about the teachings of the church so that they may decide their future using their own free will.

His philosophy of love and tolerance had been seriously tested over the past few months. Upon becoming director of the school, he quickly realized that a number of Jewish professors were already teaching in his establishment. Some had already fled the Nazi regime, including a lawyer who had previously practiced in Bavaria. He had been deported to Dachau after making an impassioned public plea against Hitler, eventually fleeing to Austria and finally to France. Others were being hunted down by the Gestapo and by Vichy's militia.

For this deeply just and tolerant man, it was abhorrent to stop providing asylum to these men whose only crime was despising Hitler and being Jewish. But Father Puech was a discreet man. He refused to get involved in politics, particularly considering that some of his students' parents were staunch defenders of the Vichy government while others were sympathetic toward the Resistance.

For this reason, he decided early on that he alone would be privy to information concerning the background of his students and staff, and he would be extremely discreet when taking on new additions to the school. Inwardly, Father Puech was horrified by the anti-Jewish measures taken by the Pétain government and particularly by the vile raids that began in 1941. As a man who believed wholeheartedly in the gospel and in loving your neighbor, there was absolutely no question for him about helping these poor souls. He decided to host several young Jewish boys and camouflage their identities, which is how he met Henri in 1943.

The boy had been forced to change his name and was now known as Henri Anglade. He had been sent to the Barral School by the principal of the Minor Seminary in Castelnaudary, who recommended him in a letter citing him as a brilliant and hard-working student.

Henri's father accompanied him to his first meeting with Father Puech. Jacob was immediately taken with the tall and pensive man who promised to watch over Henri as if he were his very own son. Based on Henri's previous test scores, the abbot decided to enroll him in the seventh grade.

The abbot made Henri swear never to reveal his true identity to anyone. Like his classmates, he would have to launch himself enthusiastically into the rigors of minor seminary and go to confession regularly. Henri was devastated by the separation from his parents and baby sister, but he understood the danger that surrounded them ever since the Germans had invaded the free zone. He promised to accept these arrangements. After Jacob had come to fetch Henri and Renee in Brout Vernet, at the end of 1940, the family had lived a happy life in Castelnaudary. Inhabitants of Castelnaudary were very hospitable and the Nazis were confined to the "occupied zone". Unfortunately, ever since the suppression of the free zone in late 1942, life for the Englanders had become considerably more complicated and degrading. Henri had even nicknamed it the "abominable transition."

Anna and Jacob were forced to separate themselves from their children. Henri was sent to the minor seminary in Castres and Renée to a convent in Limoux.

And then a miracle occurred! One night in October, Henri knelt inside the confessional and expressed his usual concerns about being separated from his family and wanting to revolt against the established order that had forced him to assume a false identity and zealously adopt a new religion. The abbot listened to the teenager's woes for a long time before asking a surprising question. "Have you become a Bar-Mitzvah, my son?" Henri was surprised by such a question, but was reassured by the complicity of the priest's words. He replied, "Yes, Father, in August of 1940, but it was a rushed affair, with only my family present." In a hushed tone, the abbot asked, "Would you like to continue your Hebrew schooling?" "Yes, Father, but that's not possible. You know that!" "Nothing is impossible, my son, if you love the Lord. Through the intervention of your parents, God has placed you under my protection. He is the God of all believers, and He doesn't necessarily want you converted to Catholicism. I can help you continue your education, if you desire it. I have phylacteries and a prayer shawl in my office that I can give to you. We could study the Tanakh together in secret. What do you say, my son?"

Henri was completely taken aback by the proposition. How could a Catholic priest come up with such a plan? But, instinctively, he trusted that this was the right thing to do. He felt compelled to form a deeper bond with religion, and with this good man who so generously wanted to pull him out of his misery and isolation. "Why not, Father! It would be wonderful. But isn't it too dangerous for you? No one must ever know that I am Jewish." "Nothing is dangerous for those who seek the light. I would be honored to teach you the scriptures in Hebrew and help you practice the faith of your ancestors!" Despite the darkness of the confessional, a beam of bright light seemed to suddenly shine inside Henri's heart. He was overwhelmed with emotion. This man speaking softly to him through the lattice was a saint! He didn't judge or threaten Henri. He simply wanted to help him along his spiritual path, no matter what his religion was.

Henri accepted the miraculous and incongruous proposition and showed up at Father Puech's office the following Thursday. The abbot ushered him in and locked the door firmly behind him. Then, after taking a seat next to Henri, he pulled out a prayer book in Hebrew, a prayer shawl, and a small box containing the phylacteries. "Today, I will teach you to wear these." He placed a small cap on the boy's head and unfolded the prayer shawl, draping it over his shoulders. Then he pulled out two black boxes hanging from leather straps. He asked Henri repeat a Hebrew benediction, then pulled Henri's sleeve back and tied the first phylactery to his arm. The second he placed on the boy's forehead.

Deeply moved, Henri felt uplifted by the ritual. Father Puech was calm and resolute. What he now did in the secrecy of his office was in full harmony with his faith and his deepest beliefs. His objective was not to create converts or future priests, but to bring these young souls closer to God. Though slightly unorthodox, helping Henri was an affirmation of the beliefs that Father Puech wanted to share with others: the freedom to believe in God, no matter one's faith, and the importance of loving one's neighbor.

The light filtering through the window is fading slowly into the shadows of the waning afternoon. It is almost five o'clock in the evening. Father Puech turns on his desk lamp so they can finish their reading. Thousand-year old phrases from the Bible light up before their very eyes.

Just as Abraham is about to commit the irreparable, his arm is stopped by a divine angel. His son, Isaac, is replaced on the sacrificial altar by a ram caught in the bushes nearby. Abraham's trust in the Lord was not in vain after all.

The abbot stops reading at this point and leans toward Henri. "You see, my son, you must have faith in the path that God has laid out for you. I know that you and your family are suffering right now but, just like Abraham, you will also meet an angel who reunites you with your family when this war comes to an end. Now, it's getting late. We'll stop here. Take off your shawl and your phylacteries. We'll continue this in two weeks."

Henri takes everything off without a word and bids the abbot good night before leaving his office. He still doesn't understand why Father Puech is facilitating his practice of his faith in private, but it has given him a profound inner peace and a renewed trust in mankind. Father Puech is right. Despite these harsh times, an angel will come save them: him, Renée, and his parents. He's sure of it.

CHAPTER 7
1944
THE ARREST OF JACOB ENGLANDER
RENÉE

It is late July and everyone sits at the table around a delicious stew that Anna has prepared. Henri and Renée are there, along with their friends, the Eisenbachs, and Anna's little sister, Hélène. It was Hélène who helped them find this little house in Querbes, near Capdenac, in the Aveyron. The "Boches" – a disparaging term for German soldiers – will not come here. They are too preoccupied with the Allies who just took Normandy and are headed for Provence.

Renée read about it in the newspaper, along with her brother. She is happy to be back amongst her family after the months of strife, of hypocrisy, and lies that she just spent under a false identity. And yet she cannot be at peace. Her beloved father, Jacob, is not at the table and no one knows if he will ever be seen again. As Alphonse de Lamartine said, "When one person is missing, the whole world seems empty."

After retrieving her from the convent where she had been in hiding, Renée's mother told her the story of her father's arrest in February of 1944 innumerable times. Anna was still punishing herself for letting him go to the house on the rue de la Comédie that awful night.

Towards the end of 1943, after placing Henri and Renee in the hands of Catholic institutions and changing their last names from Englander to Anglade, Anna and Jacob quickly realized that living on the rue de la Comédie, in the middle of Castelnaudary, had become too dangerous. Their strong German accents singled them out as refugees, and the French administration was becoming increasingly bureaucratic and intolerant. Jacob had also made the mistake of officially declaring himself as a "Jew" at the town hall, overly eager to respect the requirements of the French Republic.

My Mother Renée ID at age 7, mentioning her Jewish origin

SÛRETÉ NATIONALE

Commissariat de Police
de
CASTELNAUDARY

CERTIFICAT

D'IDENTITE

Nous FERIS René

Commissaire de Police de la Ville de Castelnaudary,

Certifions, après enquête :

que Melle ENGLANDER Renée, demeurant à CASTELNAUDARY Rue de la Comédie, de nationalité Française et de confession Israélite

est née à Paris

le 25 Février 1936

fille de Jakob

et de HOLZER Chana

Castelnaudary, le 3 Mars 1943.

LE COMMISSAIRE DE POLICE.

Renée loathed the French identification certificate that her father had filled out at the beginning of 1943 in Castelnaudary. She especially hated the words "of Jewish faith" written next to the picture of a visibly frightened seven-year old. How outrageous!

Jacob took his boss, Mr. Bonnefont, into his confidence. He, in turn, introduced him to his notary, Mr. Gouttes. A local bigwig in his fifties, Mr. Gouttes hated the occupying Nazis and could not tolerate the servility of the Vichy regime. Not only had it surrendered to the enemy, but it even collaborated actively with them, handing over innocent Jews and happily sending the majority of the French youth to do compulsory work service (STO).

Mr. Gouttes was a proud man, descended from a long line of Chauriens – inhabitants of Castelnaudary--who had lived in the region for centuries and were suspicious of any kind of centralized authority. He immediately befriended Jacob, the tall man with blue eyes who was trying to protect his family.

They had a shared belief in liberty and in the decent men who worked hard to build a life they could be proud of. Mr. Gouttes understood the family's delicate situation and Jacob's discomfort with living in the heart of Castelnaudary. He offered his country house in Souilhanels, a small town located a few kilometers northwest of Castelnaudary, as a refuge for Jacob and his wife.

Now Jacob had only to bike to the Bonnefont's house a few days each week to make a delivery. He was able to complete his watchmaker's work away from the shop, in the privacy of his new home in Souilhanels. He and Anna occasionally stopped by the house on the rue de la Comédie, usually at night, to pick up a few things and make sure that everything was in order

Even though Anna and Jacob were starting to lose hope, though they felt hunted like savage beasts, and though they missed their children terribly, their routine might have successfully carried them through to the end of the war.

But it all came to a screeching halt on that fateful night in January 1944, a night that would remain engraved in Anna and her children's memories until the end of their days.

Jacob had decided to go retrieve some bed sheets at their home on the rue de la Comédie. It was a particularly dark evening. Because the street was quite narrow in front of the Englander home, Anna was walking about 10 meters behind Jacob. He was about to turn the key in the lock when two Feldgendarmes came out of nowhere and called out in German, "Herr Englander?" Jacob instinctively turned around and replied, "Ya," immediately revealing his identity. Anna witnessed the scene and came to a full stop, briefly pressing up against the doorway of a house. She had the presence of mind to continue walking by as though nothing were wrong, as though she didn't know the tall man who was having an altercation with the German policemen. It was this decision that saved her life.

So it was that, to her great despair, she witnessed the arrest of her dear husband and forever lost faith in human goodness.

Jacob, surprised by the encounter, spoke a few quick words in German that Anna couldn't hear. Then, seized with panic, he tore down the narrow street that headed toward the Place de Verdun. The two Feldgendarmes were much younger and caught up to him easily in front of the fountain in the main square. They threw themselves on top of him to keep him still. Anna continued walking mechanically, like a robot, and witnessed the entire scene with ice coursing through her veins. Jacob was being handcuffed, without preamble, and carried off to God only knew where.

Anna rushed to see Mr. Gouttes, who was about to go to bed, and told him of Jacob's dreadful arrest. He calmed her down and suggested she stay the night. The next morning he went to the police station, along with Jacob's watchmaker friend, Mr. Bonnefont, to inquire about Jacob's situation. He returned bearing bad news. After spending the night in the police station, Jacob had been immediately transferred to the prison in Carcassonne. Because he was a "Jewish foreigner," the French police could do nothing to help him.

A few days later, Mr. Bonnefont obtained permission to visit Jacob in the detention center in Carcassonne. Jacob was disheveled and sported bruises that left no doubt as to the savagery of his arrest and the brutal interrogation he had surely been subjected to.

Despite their valuable connections, Mr. Gouttes and Mr. Bonnefont were powerless to do anything. The French administration was intransigent. It had been ordered to arrest all Jewish foreigners in the region and deport them to Drancy. It complied with regulations and executed these orders with apparent relish, leaving the Englander family completely dumbfounded.

Mr. Gouttes would have to be careful now. He had raised suspicions by trying too hard to save Jacob; he might even be putting Anna in further danger. The appearance of two Feldgendarmes at 29 rue de la Comédie seemed an awful lot like a trap for Anna and Jacob – a trap that had to be the result of someone's denunciation.

Anna learned that Jacob was transferred to Drancy on February 2, 1944 and then tossed onto a cattle train headed for an unknown location in Germany, on February 10, 1944. Since then, there had been no news!

Fortunately, Mr. Gouttes was there and continued to provide Anna with protection and accommodations. After collecting herself, Anna decided that she couldn't take any more and she needed to get her children back.

She made an appointment with Father Puech in Castres and told him of her troubles. The abbot advised her to wait until the end of the school year, so as not to disturb Henri's schooling. He promised to find her safe lodging nearby, where she could be near her children while she waited for the war to end. Since the Allied victories in North Africa and the German retreat on the Russian front, there was no longer any doubt that the war would be coming to an end soon.

It was Anna's baby sister, Hélène, who found the ideal haven. Hélène had immigrated to France in 1933 and had never mentioned her Jewish status. She spoke French with a perfect accent; she had gall to spare – that famous Yiddish "chutzpah"– and a lovely physique that turned many a man's head. She was hiding somewhere in the southwest of France and had succeeded previously in extracting her sister, Elsa, along with Elsa's family, from a camp in Gurs. She had also found a place for their daughter, Zelma, in a convent in Castres.

She had friends everywhere and, more importantly, friends who were partisans. They directed her to a house for rent in the region of Aveyron, in a village that fully supported the Resistance.

In May 1944, Anna went to collect Renée, then Henri, and drove toward the little town of Querbes, along with Hélène. The local population was extremely welcoming, just as the partisans had predicted. The family was able to celebrate their reunion, despite the constant loss they felt because of Jacob's arrest.

Renée is pensive tonight. She lingers over her plate for longer than usual. She feels less frightened these days and is comforted by her family's presence, and especially by her cat, Grisou, which her mother had taken care of during the long months of separation. But her horrible stay in that dreaded convent has already scarred Renée. She doesn't understand; she is only eight-years old and life has already dealt her difficult and unfair blows! Why did the German police take her father away? What had he done wrong, besides having the name Jacob and speaking French with a strong German accent? Her mother, Anna, couldn't explain it to her. Her big brother, Henri, couldn't either, despite his brilliant studies at the minor seminary in Castres. Even Aunt Hélène, who was usually a wealth of information, couldn't say where he had been taken.

Grisou is now pressed up against Renee's ankles and is purring with delight. Renée finishes her last bite of stew, petting the cat with one hand. She is lost in thought. She wishes with her entire being that she could wake up out of this nightmare and leap into the arms of her dear father!

CHAPTER 8
1949
PEACE IN JERUSALEM
ENIEQ

It is six in the morning and the sun is rising slowly over the Holy City. Enieq lies across a bag of sand, his rifle pointing east, and watches the Dome of the Rock light up little by little as if on fire. The last week of fighting has been harsh. Every meter of terrain conquered was a bitter struggle.

Enieq is so close to his goal, and yet still so far.

Before him, to his left, lies the Old City; it beckons him with open arms. He can clearly see the Dormition Abbey rising proudly from Mount Zion, an impregnable citadel protecting the southern ramparts of the Old City. The pink light of dawn is already, after only a few minutes, turning to a brilliant yellow, illuminating the rose and ochre hues of the city in all its splendor. The blocks of beige limestone, so characteristic of Jerusalem, reflect the soft warmth of the morning light.

The narrow valley below him, ripe with hundred-year old olive trees, is littered with the leftover debris of armored vehicles – a testament to the ferocity of the battle that took place here more than a year ago.

A hundred meters ahead, he can clearly see the Jordanian lines.

That damned Jordanian army! Its famous Arab Legion, in particular, was extremely well trained. They had not surrendered an inch of terrain and, more importantly, they were impeding the Israeli forces from entering the Old City! Proud, well-armed, disciplined, and weathered from fighting in the Second World War, the men of the Arab Legion had resisted the less experienced Israeli forces with unparalleled skill.

Enieq's comrades had stormed the Jaffa Gate several times, closely skirting the ramparts; but the Jordanians held their position firmly. These were professional soldiers who knew how to fight methodically and with precision.

Many times that day he had believed they were about to succeed. He and his comrades from the Haganah had managed to join forces with their fellow soldiers in the Jewish Quarter of the Old City. But the Arab Legion's counterattack, along with some very precise bombing, had forced a retreat.

They had been especially surprised by the accuracy of the snipers. He would never forget that fateful day in February when he had seen his best friend, Schmuel, fall to the ground next to him. Schmuel had been shot in the head by a bullet that came, seemingly, out of nowhere and whose aim was devilishly accurate and deadly. In vain, Enieq had tried desperately to resuscitate his friend, finally emptying the magazine of his rifle into a wall out of sheer frustration, screaming with rage.

Enieq had fought with all his might, but then understood, from the faces of the officers, that he wouldn't be going any further. He had to abandon the Old City, its Jewish Quarter, and, most especially, he had to relinquish access to the Western Wall of Herod's temple.

So near and yet so far!

Enieq was exhausted. And yet, in spite of the frustration of being thwarted in reaching a goal that was only a stone's throw away, every new day felt like a miracle. Just four short years ago, he had been a mere shadow of himself, one of the rare survivors of the Nazi death camps.

Born in 1923 in Poland, he was deported in 1941 to a labor camp after witnessing the massacre of his village. His life had been saved by his extraordinary constitution and his great skill in repairing machines. He had been forced to work in a Polish factory that manufactured crankshafts for combustion engines. Following one particular of raids from the numerous raids by the Nazis, he had nearly been executed, but the Polish factory workers petitioned the foreman to spare him. Enieq was too valuable – he alone understood the intricacies of the welding and tooling machines and was able to fix them quickly and efficiently.

How many times had Enieq intervened to unblock this or that gear? The factory workers could not operate without him. If a machine stopped working for more than an hour it could be a death warrant for its operator, whether he was Jewish or Polish or anybody else. The Nazis running the factory had no concern for human life, since the supply of subservient workers was so abundant and cost absolutely nothing. Enieq managed to survive thanks to his skill as a mechanic but he was terribly hungry and nearly starved. Throughout those long years, he had watched as all of his friends and family disappeared, one after the other. One by one, they were all taken away in the hateful covered trucks, never to be seen again. First it was his parents and his sister. Then, one night in November 1944, his brother was finally taken away. He had begged the director of the factory to help him, but it was no use. That Nazi monster had to have his quota of Jewish workers, and Enieq's brother was too feeble to be of any use to him.

When the Russians reached the labor camp adjoining the factory in 1945, Enieq was practically a ghost. He wandered the ravaged streets of Europe for six months until the Jewish Agency gave him lodging and proposed that he go to Palestine. What was a 22-year-old to do when he had already lost everything? Hence, Enieq, like so many others, set off for this unknown land but where he had at last the right to live safely as a Jew.

The Haganah quickly recognized his qualities and recruited him thanks to his determined attitude, his stocky stature (small but imposing) and, more importantly, his knack for machines. He seemed to instinctively understand how any mechanism worked, whether it was a motor, a gear, or a machine gun. He enlisted as soon as he arrived in the port of Haïfa. This life suited him. Finally, he could fight for a just cause and avenge his brothers and sisters who had been incinerated in the Nazi furnaces.

And there was the Ulpan center, where he spent his mornings learning about his new culture as well as a new language: Hebrew. It was at the Ulpan that he met Zelma, a young French woman who had also fled from Europe, a continent that had become so inhospitable to her. Like him, she was barely twenty years old. She had brilliant blue eyes, a gentle voice, and a keen intelligence. She spoke four languages fluently including Polish, German, English, and French.

She was Renée's cousin and Anna's niece – the same Zelma, now a beautiful young woman, who as a little girl had spotted the Nazis for the first time in 1933 in Mannheim.

After Jacob's deportation, Zelma and her parents, Elsa and Isaac, had tried for several years to stay in Toulouse in the southwest of France with Anna, but it was just too painful. Moreover, they had an intense fear of the French police. In 1946, they decided to leave. Life in France had become untenable. They tried staying close to Anna and her children, but they were penniless.

Isaac even tried selling American army surplus clothing on the black market but was caught by the police in November 1946 and jailed in Toulouse. He had Zelma to thank for his ultimate release. Feisty little Zelma, who had just graduated from high school with flying colors, had the incredible gall to go to the judge personally to negotiate her father's bail! He had originally set Isaac's bail at 100,000 French francs, but he was so impressed by the determination of the gutsy little lady before him and so moved by the tales of horror she told of all that her family had endured over the past five years that he finally gave in and lowered bail to 10,000 French francs. What a story! There was a lesson to be learned from this youngster who just wouldn't give up!

But 10,000 French francs was still an enormous sum – the equivalent of all the savings Isaac had put aside for Zelma to continue her studies in France. Zelma, however, did not hesitate for an instant. She convinced her mother to use their savings to pay the judge. They couldn't afford to take any more chances with the French judicial system. What if they were to begin interning Jews again, even deporting and assassinating them once more?

The lawyer defending Zelma's father was flabbergasted! How had this child managed to sway the judge? He was so impressed, he actually offered to finance her law studies and become her mentor!

But this arrest was the last straw! They couldn't stay in Europe any longer. Though it was difficult to leave Anna and her children behind, they made reservations on a cargo ship transporting goods from Marseille to Palestine. With the last bit of their savings they booked passage to Haifa, despite the increasingly intense blockade by the British navy.

The voyage was dreadful; they were trapped in the hold of the ship, squeezed between piled up cases of liquor. But the family succeeded in foiling the British and, before long, had set foot in the Holy Land. Anna and the children had immediately been taken under the wing of the Jewish Agency, which looked after their needs, including instruction in their new language at an Ulpan center.

The classes were intense. They had to decipher line after line of strange Hebrew letters that had no vowels and blended holy words from Biblical times, such as "halva," meaning milk, with words that had been invented in the 20th century, only a few years earlier, such as "mechanic", meaning automobile. Every morning, they witnessed the rebirth of the Hebrew language – a language that had been dead for two thousand years – and the rebirth of the Jewish people who, like the phoenix in ancient times, were rising slowly out of the ashes of the Holocaust.

Zelma and Enieq immediately took a shine to one another. Like the character of Gavroche in *Les Misérables*, Enieq was clever, agile, resourceful, and an orphan. Zelma was poised, exceptionally intelligent, caring, and accompanied by her two parents who immediately adopted Enieq as their son. The couple decided to marry and in December 1948, while on leave, Enieq knelt before Isaac and asked for Zelma's hand. Isaac was not surprised by the proposal. He considered Enieq a brave and capable young man and immediately gave his blessing. He sensed that this union signified the beginning of a long-awaited rebirth for their family. His only concern was that this war of independence seemed never-ending, and Enieq had been posted to the most turbulent front where vicious and violent battles were being fought: Jerusalem. Then again, Enieq had survived the worst the Nazi terrors in Poland. He must have a guardian angel! Isaac and Elsa gave the young couple their blessing and set the wedding date for June 1949.

The sun is at its highest point now. The day is particularly hot for the month of April. The light inundating the Old City has turned white, and the olive trees are still. A few birds chirp. From far away, bells toll from a cathedral inside the Old City, signaling that it is noon. For a moment, time stands still, here beneath the ramparts of Jerusalem.

Suddenly, the lieutenant leading Enieq's section appears and says, "My friends, it is done! We won't advance any further. Our commanders have decided to sign the armistice tomorrow with the Jordanians. This will now be declared a no man's land to separate our two armies. It will be the temporary border of our new country. Though we must give up on the Old City, do not be dismayed. We are alive and we are in Jerusalem!"

So near and yet so far!

Enieq does not cry. He knows that he hasn't fought in vain. The territory allocated to the Jews by the 1947 UN partition plan has increased. More importantly, they did not give up West Jerusalem, nor were they tossed into the sea as the Arab Legion, the Syrians, and the Egyptians had threatened.

Now, at last, he can build a home in Israel with Zelma, who is waiting for him in Tel Aviv. Maybe he can even follow his dream of studying engineering at the Technion, Israel's celebrated Institute of Technology!

CHAPTER 9
1965
REIMBURSING THE TRIP
MORITZ JANUARY

It is Saturday, January 16, 1965 and the old typewriter clicks away softly. Moritz, the youngest of the Holzer children, sits behind his desk, his fingers running slowly over the keys. It is three o'clock in the afternoon. Despite the snow outside, his wife has gone for tea with her friend, Linda, who lives on Queens Boulevard in the Rego Park neighborhood of New York City. Moritz loves this city that welcomed him thirty years earlier when he was fleeing the Germans. Here, the Jews live amongst themselves. Here, the Jews live in peace.

Words appear slowly on the paper:

"Dear Mr. Sandor,

When I came to America in October 1938 on the SS Washington, I purchased a round trip ticket and have never used the return portion."

Moritz is writing to the "United Lines" shipping company, with whom he bought a round-trip ticket years ago. Because he never redeemed his return ticket from America to Europe, he is hoping that he can use the credit for a new trip. His niece, Valérie Morris, has a reservation on a ship headed for Europe on February 24th. After all, a penny saved is a penny earned!

And then he remembers . . . and his eyes cloud with tears.

He was born into such a happy family, back in 1906, and that beautiful family was decimated and crushed by the war.

His parents, Wolf and Hendel, were forced out of Mannheim and back to Poland, where they were murdered in cold blood, gassed in a truck. His older brothers Samuel and Akiva suffered the same fate.

Then his sister, Regina, was arrested in France, where she had been in hiding, and deported to Auschwitz in September 1942. She never returned.

His sister, Anna, had suffered terribly. Her husband was deported to Auschwitz in February 1944 and was gassed upon arrival. Anna and her children hoped fiercely for his return after the liberation of France in 1944. Anna spent countless hours at the Lutetia Hotel trying to find him, but it was all in vain. Everything had been taken from them: her husband, the children's father, their jewelry and watch shop in Saint Denis, and even their apartment on the rue de Saintonge, which was emptied and leased to a third party. They had to wait for a decision from the civil court of the Seine in 1947 before Anna could finally get her apartment back in 1949!

And it was not until December 1955 that she finally received the official confirmation of Jacob's deportation from the French Department of Veteran Affairs.

What an indomitable spirit his sister had! Anna fought for her children to survive and ended up giving them much more. Thanks to his mother's encouragement, Henri went on to study medicine and excelled at his studies. He briefly considered moving to the United States as well, but could not leave his mother and sister. Little Renée also overcame her painful past and earned a baccalaureate – the French high school diploma – in 1955 followed by a bachelor's degree in child psychology in 1959. More importantly, she met a young Jewish man from Tunisia and they married in 1959. It was difficult for Anna to accept this "mixed" marriage to a North African Jew whose accent garbled the pronunciation of the Hebrew prayers. But he was so charming, so intelligent – he was studying medicine – and so considerate of Renée that Anna, and especially, Henri, finally accepted him into the family. In 1963 he gave Renée a son they named Jacques in honor of Jacob's memory.

Thanks to fate, or perhaps luck, the three remaining sisters – Elsa, Marie, and Hélène – also survived and immigrated to Israel where they now live in peace.

Moritz is a survivor. He was lucky to leave for the United States at the very last second. He was spared the Nazi hell. He found the love of his life and learned a fine trade, upholstery, creating armchairs and sofas that enabled him to support his family for more than twenty years.

Words and memories float onto the page:

"I believe I should also call your attention to the fact that the original ticket was lost long ago. If it is necessary for me to sign papers regarding the loss of the ticket, as well as transfer forms to Miss Morris, please be good enough to send them to me. "

He'll send the letter on Monday.

PART II

THE SILBERMAN FAMILY

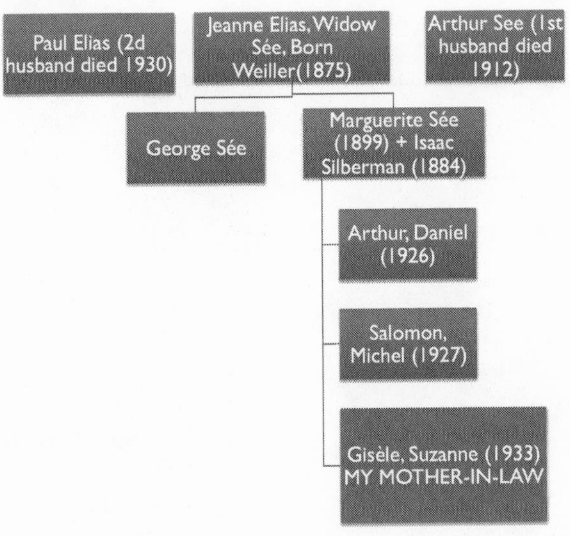

CHAPTER 10
1938
VACATION IN TROUVILLE
JEANNE

Jeanne is furious. She arrived at the St. Lazare station in Paris an hour ago and has been waiting for her idiot son-in-law to arrive ever since. Little five year old Gisèle grasps her grandmother's hand and is also impatient. "What are Mommy and Daddy up to?" she asks. "I don't know, sweetie; your father is always late and it's getting quite frustrating!" It is early afternoon on July 1st, and the great hall of the train station is beginning to get unbearably hot as throngs of excited Parisians hurry along, finally heading off on their annual vacation and eager to reach the seaside. The overwhelming din results from people everywhere jostling each other, yelling to companions, and whistling! The steam from the locomotives only intensifies the humidity in the hot summer air. The atmosphere is almost excrutiating.

Jeanne Elias, born Weiler, "Widow Sée," as they used to say, is elegantly dressed, as was her way. She carries herself with grace, poise, and dignity, her posture ramrod straight despite her sixty-three years. Her long blond hair is pulled back in a perfect bun and tucked under a large hat reserved for special occasions., Her makeup is tastefully done. She has deliberately chosen to wear her impressive opal-green Dior dress suit and high-heeled shoes, which give her the height advantage needed to size up – or look down upon – just about anybody, especially her son-in-law. She still considers him an unkempt and uneducated foreigner that she was forced to accept into the family.

If only she hadn't needed the money, she could have waited and married her daughter to a cultured and refined Frenchman. But, at the time, she had no choice.

The death of her two successive husbands – Arthur Sée of pneumonia after the Great War and Paul Elias of a heart attack in 1924 – had left Jeanne penniless. She had expensive tastes, especially after living with her second husband in a magnificent upscale apartment in the capital. It was time to find a match for her eldest daughter – Marguerite. A suitable and wealthy match would also help ensure Jeanne's future.

At twenty-five years old, Jeanne's eldest daughter – Marguerite – possessed all the important qualities necessary for marrying well. Her financial situation forced Jeanne, however, to seek the services of her friend, Sarah Friedlander, a well-respected matchmaker, to find a suitable husband for her daughter.

Sarah had promised to find a choice prospect, a real gem, thanks to her social connections in Paris's Jewish circles.

A rare gem, indeed! Jeanne would never forget their first meeting at the Train Bleu restaurant on the second floor of the Gare de Lyon station. It was December 15, 1924. The cold was biting and, already at six in the afternoon, night had fallen, darkening the city.

Jeanne had arrived early with Sarah and Marguerite to ensure good seating for the important occasion. The maitre'd led them to a table at the back of the restaurant that faced a large bay window overlooking the station square. A magnificent chandelier sparkled overhead. Marguerite was more beautiful than ever, with large turquoise eyes that Sarah had highlighted with subtle makeup. She wore a ruffled pink and white dress. Jeanne was delighted with the overall effect.

Around seven o'clock, the maitre'd led Isaac Silberman to join the ladies at the table. Isaac gave them each a customary kiss on the hand. He was not at all bad looking and his chestnut eyes had a mischievous twinkle behind his round glasses. However, he had two major flaws: he was 15 years older than Marguerite and had traces of a dreadful Romanian accent that made him sound like a vulgar gypsy.

The meal proceeded smoothly despite the fact that Jeanne had a terrible time finding suitable topics of conversation to engage in with such an uncouth character. Isaac was from Romania and had moved to Paris after the Great War to build a new life for himself. He had changed his name from "Argentarum" to "Silberman" in an attempt to sound more French. How ridiculous, thought Jeanne. He certainly appeared to have a flare for business, though, and had opened a watch and jewelry shop in 1922 – the "Cadran" (Watch Face) specializing in repairing watches, clocks, and jewelry and located at 29 rue Vieille du Temple in the heart of the Paris Jewish neighborhood.

Business had been good and he had accumulated enough capital to start a family. He was immediately taken with Marguerite's youthful charm and dazzling smile, and she was attracted to him as well. Despite his accent and his country bumpkin manners, she liked his strength of character, which seemed to be a trademark of all hard-working immigrants, and was intrigued by the mystery surrounding the life he had left behind. He was also quite funny! She laughed uproariously when, toward the end of the meal, he downed the liquid from the finger bowl in one gulp thinking it was a palette cleanser before dessert. Jeanne couldn't hide a little gasp of horror that instinctively passed her lips, but Marguerite burst out laughing before explaining her mother's reaction to him. When Isaac fell all over himself apologizing, his sheepish air amused her all the more.

The following day, Isaac asked Marguerite out for coffee, and the courtship progressed rapidly. Jeanne was reluctant to agree to the marriage, but Sarah was persuasive citing Isaac's increasing wealth: he had a solid reputation as a watchmaker-jeweler, a loyal client base, and his business would only continue to prosper. What's more, he made Marguerite laugh. What more could one ask for? Against her better judgment, Jeanne eventually softened, agreeing to their union. They were married on June 25, 1925 at the town hall in the 20th arrondissement, with an elaborate celebration immediately following at the Synagogue de la Victoire.

Sarah often had to remind Jeanne that there was nothing regrettable about this union. Isaac and Marguerite had given her three adorable grandchildren – Daniel in 1926, Michel in 1927, and little Gisèle in 1933. And as Sarah has predicted, Isaac had a true flare for business and managed to provide quite generously for his family. He and Marguerite had moved into a lovely three-bedroom apartment on the rue du Cambodge, near the Place Gambetta in the 20th arrondissement. He had also rented a charming two-bedroom flat for Jeanne just a block away on rue des Gâtines. In return, he merely asked that Jeanne help Marguerite care for the younger children. Jeanne was not displeased by this arrangement. She loved her grandchildren, particularly little Gisèle, whom she had been caring for since her birth. Jeanne had practically raised the child herself. At age five, Gisèle already knew how to read, thanks to nightly lessons from Jeanne. Gisèle spent most of her free time with her grandmother, whom she admired greatly. Gisele even had her own bedroom at her grandmother's apartment.

Every summer since 1935, Isaac would rent a beachfront house in the little town of Trouville off the Normandy coast during the months of July and August. Jeanne adored these wonderful holidays with Marguerite and her children. She loved Trouville for its fish market, its narrow streets, and the mild weather that was neither too hot nor too cold. And, of course, there was the beach. Isaac always rented a canopy and lawn chairs for them with a stunning view of the English Channel. The location was ideal: it was close to the ice cream stand and near enough to the beach that Jeanne could keep an eye on the children while they played. Their favorite pastime was frolicking in the puddles formed by the retreating tide and building sandcastles that would inevitably get swept away when the tide returned.

Jeanne developed a summer routine and even became friends with her neighbors in the next beach tent over. The German couple came to Trouville every summer with their son, who was about Daniel's age. They were refined people, unlike Isaac. The husband spoke near-perfect French and his wife loved playing chess, the very game that Jeanne adored. They never discussed politics; Jeanne always tried to avoid sensitive topics and really couldn't fathom how such polite and distinguished people could put up with Hitler's racist, fascist policies. Those two summer months in the invigorating sea air were Jeanne's joy and delight, and she cherished the long lazy days spent with Marguerite and her precious grandchildren.

Jeanne finally spots her son-in-law. He arrives out of breath, as is usually the case, accompanied by Marguerite and the two boys. She sizes him up once before falling into the kind of silent rage of which only sheis capable. "This is unacceptable! Isaac, you are always late. Poor little Gisèle is withering in this heat and we still don't have our train tickets. Did you forget to purchase them?" Isaac is exasperated by Jeanne's usual sharp tongue and condescending attitude, particularly considering that he pays for everything, but offers his apologies nonetheless. There was an emergency at the shop and, after all, business must come first. He reaches into his pocket and hands Jeanne the train tickets. They must hurry; the train is leaving in ten minutes! The little group runs toward the train, barely reaching the door in time, and jumps onboard at the very last minute. Isaac helps them onto the train and lifts the three heavy suitcases up from the platform, storing them in the luggage hold. Jeanne, Marguerite, and the children find their compartment and merrily sink into the comfortable seats. Isaac has just enough time to hastily disembark the train, with the conductor shooting him a reprimanding look as he whistles out the departure warning.

Isaac is finally alone on the platform and relieved to see his family – and his mother-in-law in particular – pull away from the quay. Daniel and Michel lean out of their compartment window to blow him kisses.

The long-awaited vacation to Trouville has finally begun.

CHAPTER 11
1942
HUNTED DOWN IN PARIS
DANIEL

The waiting is unbearable. Daniel squeezes up against the white tiles lining the walls of the Paris metro. Despite the July heat, he is cold. Petrified, he struggles to catch his breath. It is mid-morning, and the crowd is sparse in the République Metro station. Daniel doesn't dare move. He waits patiently for the subway that will take him to the Gare de Lyon train station. He is wearing a stylish checkered jacket with a cap pulled low over his forehead so that no one will recognize him.

Don't draw attention to yourself! Whatever you do, do not get caught!

He carries a faded leather satchel, worn from years of use, in which he has packed a few of his favorite books. He is no longer wearing the infamous yellow star that was sewn onto his chest just a few days ago. He hasn't worn it since Commissioner Collet, the chief of police of the Place Gambetta and a close friend of his grandmother, Jeanne, visited their apartment on rue du Cambodge to deliver terrible news.

The commissioner had called Isaac at his shop on the rue Vieille du Temple to inform him that he would be stopping by Isaac's home that evening around eight o'clock. The commissioner was greeted by Marguerite, Isaac, Jeanne, and Daniel, who, at the age of sixteen, was now permitted to participate in adult discussions. They all sat down to talk at the dining room table while Michel looked after his little sister, Gisèle, in the adjacent bedroom.

"Mr. and Mrs. Silberman, Mrs. Elias, I need to warn you that something terrible is about to happen," the Commissioner whispered while wrapping his hands around the mug of hot tea that Marguerite had poured for him. "You are no longer safe here, in Paris. A vast operation is being mounted to round up all Jews and hand them over to the Nazis. You are on this list. Your family—the Silbermans! Fortunately, I was able to remove Mrs. Elias from the list because of her French ancestry, but I cannot do this for your family, Mr. Silberman, because you are considered foreigners. You must leave immediately and head somewhere safe. You must not speak of this to anyone. My very life depends on it. I loathe this war, but I cannot do anything to stop it. In a few days, I'll be forced to return to this street and arrest you all. You must leave now; I beg you!"

Jeanne did not move but tears dropped silently from her knowing blue eyes and rolled slowly down her cheeks. Marguerite remained stoic, unable to say a word, petrified by what she was hearing. Isaac also maintained a dignified front, though inside he was seething with rage. How could the country that gave birth to human rights sink so low and accept the unacceptable by arresting its children and delivering them to the enemy? "Are you sure of this, Commissioner? Is the situation so dire? Do we really need to leave?" he asked in his thick Romanian accent. "Yes, Mr. Silberman. I came to see you in person so I could impress upon you the gravity of the situation. I'm very fond of your family and cannot bear to see you arrested when you have committed no crime! Now, I must leave. No one must know that I have been here. Farewell!" He got up and affectionately embraced Isaac, Jeanne, and Marguerite before putting on his hat and overcoat. Then he was gone.

For Isaac, the moment he had been dreading for so long had finally arrived. Fortunately, he had been working on an elaborate plan for several months. He had been meticulously exchanging all his assets for diamonds, which he could easily smuggle in the seams of his jacket. Thanks to the help of his friends, Isaac had been able to rent an apartment in Nice, at 57 rue de Buffa. He had contacted a friend, Mrs. Blum, who had agreed to watch over the shop should he be forced to leave unexpectedly. He had even entrusted her with a large sum of money to continue paying the rent on his shop. Finally, he had thoroughly researched various options for crossing over the line of demarcation. He would do it near Angoulême or Châteauroux. There he could cross over without being stopped by anyone, or so he was informed. He had been told that escorts near those towns could safely smuggle people across.

The key to such an escape was to do it rapidly and without alerting the entire neighborhood, especially the landlady, a notorious gossip who had been open about her disdain for foreigners like him, The family needed to split up. Isaac would leave tomorrow; Marguerite, Daniel, and Gisèle would join him in two days. Michel would take advantage of a trip to summer camp, which had already been planned for some time, to cross over by bus. They would each bring a very small suitcase or bag with the bare necessities in order to avoid raising suspicion. Jeanne, who was not on the list, would remain a few days longer to clean up the apartments on the rue du Cambodge and rue des Gâtines and then would join them as quickly as possible. As an elderly lady who always carried herself proudly with an air of French aristocracy, she felt confident of her ability to fool the German soldiers as she traveled.

And so now Daniel finds himself alone in the République station, waiting for the subway to take him to the Gare de Lyon train station. From there, he will cross the Seine River and walk to the Gare d'Austerlitz station where his mother should be waiting for him to catch the train to Angoulême.

Don't draw attention to yourself! Do not get caught!

Finally, the subway train pulls up with a screeching halt and stops in front of him. Daniel walks slowly but confidently toward a middle car, releases the latch, and gets in.

He hadn't set foot in one of these subway cars in weeks, not since the infamous incident at the beginning of June. Running late as usual, he had been rushing to get to the Maison Palazzi on rue Rambuteau where he worked as a jeweler's apprentice. In his haste, he had accidentally boarded a subway car forbidden to Jews. As the train rumbled toward the next station, a German officer approached Daniel. Inspecting him with a nasty expression, the soldier grabbed him by the collar and sneered, "You aren't allowed in here, Jew!" The man had seized him roughly, ready to toss him from the car at the next station. Just as Daniel was being unceremoniously ejected from the train, he caught the eye of an elegantly dressed woman wearing a large hat. Her narrowed black eyes threw darts at him as she cried, "That's exactly what you deserve!" He felt such disgust at that instant for the yellow star he had been forced to wear ever since the German decree of May 29, 1942.

He had witnessed the escalation of rampant anti-Semitism throughout his adolescence. It had begun with snide comments from his classmates at the rue Sorbier primary school. Suddenly, he was fending off attacks from Didier, who called him a dirty Jew and had even struck him once at recess, landing them both in the principal's office.

The situation had worsened ever since the French capitulation with the enforcing of Marshal Pétain's discriminatory laws. Daniel was no longer permitted to go to the Square Edouard Vaillant in front of the Tenon Hospital, near his apartment on rue du Cambodge. Daniel loved the park's green expanses and the tranquility it provided. He had often gone there to clear his head or listen to the small orchestra that played every evening at six o'clock in the gazebo. And then there was Denise, a classmate whom he had adored ever since he first met her in eighth grade. Her carefree spirit, her chestnut eyes, and her charming smile had utterly enchanted him. She was so vivacious, so intelligent! With her at his side, he felt like he could take on the world! Together, they joked about their professors and spent hours talking about everything and nothing at all. And then, in ninth grade, just before final exams, they had shared a magical moment when, sitting on a bench in the park, he had taken her hand and kissed her gently on the lips.

Sadly, however, everything had changed in the fall of 1940, with the new regulations in place. A cruel sign had been posted in front of the park entrance stating, "Forbidden to Jews!" He hadn't seen Denise since their final exams that July and the beginning of his apprenticeship in the Palazzi house. How terrified she must have been of these Jews that everyone was denouncing so vehemently!

Finally, the subway train pulls into the Gare de Lyon station. Daniel exits and climbs the stairs as calmly as possible until he is aboveground, out in the fresh air on the boulevard Diderot. He avoids the gaze of passersby, particularly German soldiers. He walks slowly along the Austerlitz Bridge, risking a quick glance at the magnificent view offered by Paris and the Seine. When will he be able to come back here? He doesn't know. And suddenly the fear of the unknown that he has been keeping at bay for so long threatens to choke him.

Don't draw attention to yourself! Whatever you do, do not get caught!

He reaches the Left Bank and heads toward the Austerlitz station, speeding up as he takes the stairs toward the entrance. Next, he must find his mother, Marguerite, who is waiting for him under the giant clock. Finally, he spots her! What a relief! There she is, holding Gisèle by the hand. She has packed only a small handbag so as not to attract attention. As planned, they do not acknowledge one another but head directly toward the train for Angoulême. His mother passes him by and slips him his ticket without saying a word. They get on the train. It is full of German soldiers. How terrifying! Daniel can't find an empty seat and decides to stand in the aisle. Meanwhile, Gisèle and Marguerite manage to find spots in a compartment in the next car down from his.

Daniel tries to calm his nerves by burying himself in one of his favorite books: Victor Hugo's *Les Misérables.* It's a profound book, beautifully written, and it affords him some escape, at least for a little while. Finally, the train slowly starts moving away from the platform. The conductor comes by and silently stamps his ticket. Daniel has never been very religious and he doesn't know how to pray. He closes his eyes for a long while and wonders what the future holds and whether the fear that now overwhelms him will ever truly go away.

CHAPTER 12
1942
THE DISAPPEARANCE OF JEANNE MARGUERITE

CARTE POSTALE
EXPÉDITEUR
DESTINATAIRE

CARTE POSTALE
EXPÉDITEUR
DESTINATAIRE

Postcards sent from prisons by Jeanne to Marguerite in August 1942, just after her arrest.

"Just a quick note to let you know that they are moving us to an unknown location. Please do not fret if you don't hear from me for a while and pass this message along to my children and friends. I'll send word just as soon as I can. I am so desperately miserable and distraught – someone has got to take me seriously and help me! Give everyone a kiss for me and inform Margot as soon as possible. (I feel like I'm losing my mind, as anybody would here!) Don't send anything until further notice. They've freed everyone over seventy years old. Unfortunately, I'm only sixty-eight. Tell Georges he must hurry. I'm begging him! Your dear friend and mother."

Marguerite can't stop rereading these words, "chicken scratch" scrawled in blue ink onto a postcard by Mrs. Blum, her contact in Paris. She had hastily transcribed the last bit of news that she received from Jeanne – words that Jeanne had written from the Pithiviers internment camp.

Marguerite feels incredibly alone, here in their new apartment on the rue de la Buffa in Nice. The gentle light of December, reflecting off the building across the street, floods her dining room as she sits and reads the postcard dated September 27, 1942. She reads it over and over again, losing herself in her mother's last words.

Little Gisèle is in the room next-door, quietly absorbed in her abridged version of Victor Hugo's *Les Misérables.* Her brother, Daniel, gave her the book for her birthday. "It's my favorite book. You're going to love it; you'll see," he told her. "It's a beautiful story: the story of a man who is very unhappy but has such a big heart!" She has just reached her favorite part of the book, when Jean Valjean takes Cosette's hand to help her carry her bucket of water back from the well. Gisele is so enthralled by the wonderful story that she doesn't hear her mother's sobbing.

The boys have gone to the beach and Isaac is discussing business at a café with friends. He is looking into better ways of profiting from his diamonds to ensure his family's survival until the end of the war.

Where is Jeanne? Where have they taken her? Why doesn't she send news? Marguerite feels like she is also losing her sanity.

It had all started off so well. They had been incredibly lucky when fleeing to the free zone.

Isaac made it through first, near Châteauroux, without any complications, bribing the necessary people with a few diamonds.

As planned, Michel crossed over the line of demarcation separately, on a school trip to a summer camp in the south of France. The bus full of teenagers stopped at the border post in the south of Bourges and a German soldier came on board to inspect everyone's identification cards. Michel handed him his ID. His full name, Salomon Silberman (Michel was actually his middle name) left no doubt as to his Jewish origins. The soldier hesitated and looked into his eyes for a long time. Michel did not let himself be intimidated. He gave the German deputy officer a proud stare befitting a fifteen-year-old adolescent. Was it his youthful pride or the soldier's own humanity that saved Michel's life? No one will ever know. But the officer handed back Michel's identification card without a word and didn't try to stop him. Once the barrier of the customs border was lifted, the bus resumed its trek toward the free zone without problems.

The flight to the south was less smooth for Marguerite, Daniel, and little Gisèle. Their train left the Austerlitz station and headed slowly toward Angoulême. For the duration of the trip, Marguerite had to endure the crude banter and coarse laughter of four German officers seated in her train compartment. She struggled to conceal her concern for her family and especially for Daniel, who, she knew, was crouched down somewhere in a nearby train car. She distracted herself from her worry by delving into a complicated knitting project – a wool scarf that only she knew the pattern for. She enjoyed knitting very much. It was a useful hobby and, in this case, it successfully kept her mind off her unbearable neighbors and helped shield her disgust for them. Meanwhile, Gisèle was absorbed in an illustrated edition of *The Last of the Mohicans.* She was enchanted with its tales of Native Americans. At nine years old, she sensed that something was awry but could not quite put her finger on it. She was more amused than anything by the German soldiers who spoke so boisterously and winked at her.

More than eight hours later, the train finally pulled into the Angoulême station. Marguerite did not idle when getting off the train; pulling Gisèle firmly out of her reverie, Marguerite made her way quickly to the station café where to reunite with Daniel. Phew! There he was, his complexion pallid, toting his leather satchel. They met discreetly, with no show of demonstrative affection, and headed toward the Oiseau Bleu Inn, on the outskirts of town, where they would spend the night.

Isaac had arranged everything ahead of time. Through his network of friends, he had transferred sufficient funds for Mr. Reynard, the owner of the Oiseau Bleu Inn, to care for Marguerite, Daniel, and Gisèle. The innkeeper treated them kindly and made them feel welcome. The family felt better for the first time in two days, warmed by Mrs. Reynard's stew and the hospitality they were being shown.

The following day, they slept late, then prepared for the great adventure that awaited them. Mrs. Reynard drove to a neighboring farm where Marguerite, Daniel, and Gisele joined a group of thirty people, mostly women and children, who had also decided to cross the line of demarcation. Around midnight, a guide arrived to smuggle the group across and their trek along the backcountry roads began. There was no moon that night and they took cautious steps in the darkness. Listless black shapes swayed in the wind – the only indication of the rows of trees lining the fields. Though it was a mild night in July, Gisèle and Daniel were both trembling. Their shoes pinched their feet. A storm the night before had left the roads slick and sodden with rain, and mud clung to them. Just as they came upon a paved road, the guide suddenly signaled for them to lie down in a nearby ditch; he had spotted a patrol of German soldiers on bicycles. The two soldiers did not notice the fugitives as they pedaled by and the group eventually resumed its difficult trek.

At last, around four o'clock in the morning, they reached the town of Bouex, the last village before reaching the line of demarcation. They needed to hurry, for they only had two hours left before sunrise.

They walked in single-file along a forest path that cut through a wood, the obstacle between the group and the village of Vouzan on the other side of the line. They had to hold hands in the pitch black. Their leader moved slowly, stopping the group every fifteen minutes to listen for the sound of men on patrol. Marguerite, Daniel, and Gisèle held on tightly to each other's hands, their hearts in their throats, hoping that the terrifying ordeal would end as quickly as possible. Suddenly, they came upon a clearing. In fact, it was a shallow trench that cut across the forest along the line of demarcation. The guide inspected the clearing for a long while before finally concluding that the time was right and ushered the group rapidly across. Daniel noticed posts planted along the furrow, every few meters, for as far as the eye could see. They were striped in the Nazis colors—red, white, and black. "This is it? This is the dreaded line? There's not even any barbed wire!" thought Daniel. They made it to the other side quickly and continued their journey through the forest.

The last few kilometers were the most difficult. The younger children in the group were exhausted. Some grimaced in pain; others sobbed silently.

Dawn was approaching, and it was imperative not to be caught. Even the French border police took cruel pleasure in catching escaping Jews and putting them in internment camps in the free zone.

They finally arrived, drained and exhausted, in the little town of Vouzan where a group of farmers welcomed and fed them. They were saved! They were safe! Marguerite hugged Daniel and Gisèle tightly for a long time. They were tired, but elated. Isaac's plan, and his diamonds, had paid off. More importantly, he had put them in the hands of a reliable guide.

The remainder of the trip was much less stressful. They took four buses in succession: one to Périgueux, another to Toulouse, a third to Montpellier and the last one, finally, to Nice. They were joyfully reunited with Isaac and Michel and took up residence in their magnificent apartment at number 57 rue de la Buffa.

The apartment was large and stately, located on the third floor of a beautiful building of white cut stone at the corner of the rue de la Buffa and rue de Rivoli. It was very spacious, with large, high windows that faced due north, bathing the home with soft white light that reflected off the building across the street.

Daniel and Michel immediately fell in love with their new home. The weather was ideal and the beach was only a hundred yards away! It took only five minutes to walk down the rue de Rivoli and there was the magnificent Promenade des Anglais, lined with majestic palm trees and just across from the impressive Hôtel Negresco, which seemed to dominate the beachfront with its imposing pink and green dome.

Daniel and Michel headed off to the beach every morning. They spent hours walking along the Promenade and admiring the beautiful young women as they strolled leisurely, their slender figures fetchingly highlighted by their colorful dresses.

They had nothing left to fear from the Germans. The occupying army in Nice was Italian, whose attitude was much more relaxed. They even favored the protection of the Jews, to the great displeasure of their Nazi allies. What a contrast to the Parisian hell they had endured during the previous months!

Despite the joy of being reunited under Nice's sunny skies, the family remained haunted by Jeanne's disappearance. What could have happened to her? Marguerite was going mad, reliving those nightmarish days in August over and over again in her mind.

Everything had been planned perfectly. Jeanne would cross the line of demarcation on her own, following the same route Marguerite and her children had taken a few days earlier. But unlike for Marguerite, something went awry and Jeanne was captured.

Marguerite learned of these misfortunes from a postcard that Jeanne sent her on August 1st from the prison in Angoulême:

"I was captured not ten meters from the line of demarcation. And now I'm here. I don't know for how long! This is killing me. I don't know what to do or how long I can stand it. Nobody knows what they plan on doing with us…You can imagine, my dear child, what I must be going through. I need for you get some things together and send me a parcel. But wait a bit – they plan on moving us soon. I'll let you know as soon as it's possible to send mail. You must send it express, for there is absolutely nothing to eat here. I don't even know when I'll see you again. Sending you all my love, Your Mother. Give my little Gisèle a hug and tell her that I love her."

Marguerite was submerged in despair. How horrible! What could she do? Isaac had immediately taken action and contacted Mrs. Blum in Paris. Before leaving the capital, he had entrusted her with a large sum of money to keep paying the rent on his apartment, his shop, and Jeanne's apartment as well. Now they needed to send provisions to Jeanne. She was elderly and wouldn't last long sleeping on straw mats and eating only the meager rations provided by the prison. The second card from Jeanne, sent from a prison in Poitiers, was no more reassuring:

"You've no doubt received my letter describing the misfortune that's befallen me. I have no idea when it will end. There is no more consideration for the French or the elderly. We are being moved from this camp to Drancy. Can you believe it? You know how much I dreaded that place, and now to find out that I'm headed there. It's devastating."

So she was being moved to Drancy, that horrific internment facility located in the suburbs to the east of Paris. The majority of Jews rounded up during raids in France ended up going through Drancy, under the supervision of French police who answered to the German authority.

Drancy was reputed to maintain its prisoners under abominable conditions. Rumors abounded about that the director of the camp, a Nazi psychopath who took sick pleasure in starving his prisoners. There were tales of sealed railroad cars leaving the station of Bourget-Drancy with thousands of prisoners aboard. Their destination was Germany and its abhorrent labor camps. But what paralyzed Marguerite with dread was that, unlike the French internment camps where one could exchange letters with the prisoners, once someone was transported to Germany, they were never heard from again! Communication stopped completely! Some said that the infamous German labor camps were actually sites designed for the wholesale extermination of Jews. There were even horror stories of mass executions by firing squads in front of open trenches. Some stories went so far as to suggest that Jews were being put to death by lethal gas. Most French Jews thought this preposterous; such mass murder could not possibly be true!

On August 20th a card finally arrived from Jeanne in Drancy. She updated the family on her situation and, most importantly, gave them an address for mailing her care package:

"My dear child, Today is the only day that I can write to you. We are only permitted to send mail once every 15 days, and we are allowed to receive one package. You have to put it together for me as best you can. You must send it to the following address: IJIF, 20 boulevard de Belleville, Paris. For Mrs. Elias, Drancy Camp, Block 3, Room 4. Send me as much food as possible. I'm so hungry. Ask everyone to help you and make sure to write to Simon about my situation. Tell him not to forget his aunt. You can send tomatoes (not too ripe), olives, cheese, fruit, canned goods, etc."

Sadly, the news of her health was not encouraging:

"I am currently in the infirmary. This whole calamity has made me sick. They thought I might have pneumonia, but now I'm doing a bit better. They're giving me massages to help with my stress. I am alarmingly thin! I weigh 110 pounds. It all stems from the anxiety, of course; I am truly miserable. How could such a catastrophe happen to me? Martha is here with me; I think I already told you that. I can't elaborate any further but I do so hope to see you all very soon. Please send news of everyone. I cry every day thinking how far away I am from my family. I had so been looking forward to spending time with you all and having a rest. And what must my dear little Gisèle be saying? How she must miss me."

Jeanne was right. Little Gisèle asked for her often. She didn't understand the separation from the beloved Grandma who had raised her until now and whom she admired so. Gisele missed the scent of her grandmother's perfume; she missed her regal air and the dignified way she carried herself like a great lady. She didn't understand why her mother was so worried or why she spent so many hours staring at Grandma's postcards. And why had the French policemen arrested Grandma anyway? What had she done wrong?

These were difficult things to explain to a nine-year-old, and Marguerite struggled to answer her little girl.

Thanks to Mrs. Blum, Marguerite managed to send a large parcel of provisions to her mother. In mid-September, she learned that Jeanne had been transferred to the Pithiviers camp. She received a last postcard dated September 27, and, after that, nothing . . .

The afternoon light was slowly fading on this short day in December.

Marguerite wipes away her tears. She needs to pull herself together. She needs to take care of Gisèle and help Isaac through this ordeal. She hears Daniel and Michel climbing the stairs four at a time. They are returning from their escapades on the Promenade des Anglais and it's time to get supper ready. Marguerite carefully tucks the September 27 postcard into a small notebook and slides it into the drawer of her buffet.

Where is Jeanne? Where have they taken her? Why doesn't she write? Marguerite is mad with worry.

CHAPTER 13
1944
THE ESCAPE
GISÈLE

That's it – it's decided! Tonight, Gisèle will leave this hellhole. She can no longer endure the cruelty and spitefulness in this house. She doesn't want to have anything to do with these monsters! It is ten o'clock at night and the masters of the house have gone to bed. She hides in the tiny attic that serves as her bedroom and quietly packs her suitcase. She doesn't want to raise suspicion. She folds a few pieces of clothing. She won't need to bring very much; it's late August and the weather is still mild on this farm nestled deep in la Touraine, a region along the Loire valley.

The ten-year-old trembles nervously; she has never run away before. But tonight, it's decided. She's going to leave this farm and its horrible inhabitants: the awful father who made her do so many chores in the barn and who beat her several times with his belt, his monstrous wife, Josette, who is anti-Semitic to the tips of her fingernails and treats Gisèle like an animal. Worst of all is their 22-year-old son, Fernand, who is enrolled in the militia and looks at her with leering eyes. He puts his hands on her bottom every time he gets the chance. She loathes them all to the very depths of her soul!

Unlike in her favorite book *Les Misérables*, Gisele knows there is no Jean Valjean to save her. She needs to free herself from the Thénardier household and find her parents in Nice. They must have been freed by now, as the Allies landed in Provence and already reached the capital. She heard about it on the radio this past week and, though Ferdinand claimed that the Germans would effortlessly fend off the attack, she saw the fear in his mother's eyes. She understands that France is about to be liberated.

The nights are punctuated more and more frequently by the shrill sirens of the neighboring town and by the glow from the Allies' bombs that drop indiscriminately on railways, in fields, and on the town hall. Gisèle may only be ten years old, but the last two years of misery have matured her beyond her years. She senses that the end of the war is near.

By the light of a small candle, Gisele carefully packs her few belongings – her beloved rag doll, her copy of *Les Misérables* that she has read so many times, and the diary in which she has confided her sorrows every night since that dreadful day in September 1943 when the Nazis invaded Nice.

Since arriving in Nice a year ago, Gisèle's life had been completely derailed. Her dear Grandma Jeanne had been transported to a labor camp in Germany. Gisèle had waited for her for so long! She missed everything about Jeanne – her caresses, her soft but authoritarian tone, her enchanting perfume, her hats, and even her stern lectures!

Gisèle ached every time her mother cried after receiving a postcard from Paris confirming that Jeanne would not be returning from the labor camp. Gisèle did not see her father very much; he was busy monetizing his diamonds to help the family survive. As for her brothers, they were just a couple of idiots who spent their days ogling girls on the "Promenade des Anglais".

She would have liked to go to school but her mother was too devastated and her father too preoccupied to take the necessary steps to enroll her. Furthermore, Isaac did not want to draw undue attention to the family by sending Gisèle to school in the middle of the first trimester. And so they had decided to wait until the beginning of the next school year, in 1943, to put Gisèle back in school.

But, suddenly, in 1943, the Germans came to replace the Italians and the hunt for Jews was renewed. Just as before, it was Isaac who made the decisions and plotted ways to protect his family. Daniel, Michel, Gisèle, Isaac, and Marguerite would have to separate. The boys were sent to the Don Bosco Catholic Institute in Nice. Gisèle joined a convent of Catholic nuns, near Cannes. The parents hid with non-Jewish friends in Nice.

That was how Gisèle ended up, at the beginning of October 1943, in the care of nuns and living in a convent.

She spent six months there, long enough to develop a revulsion toward anything resembling a cross for the rest of her days. The Mother Superior was a horrible woman. She did nothing but shout all the time! Fortunately, Sister Alice was the one in charge of their dorms. She taught Gisèle to recite the morning and evening prayers so that no one would suspect she was Jewish. According to the papers her father arranged to be made for her, her name was no longer Gisèle Silberman but Gisèle Guilbert.

She loathed the convent, which was run rigidly by the Mother Superior. Everything here irritated Gisèle. Classes were taught by Sister Caroline, who filled the students' heads with the incomprehensible catechism. The cafeteria food was repugnant. Gisèle was unsure if this was a result of the war or of the pure incompetence of the sisters in the kitchen. She couldn't stand the soups made of stunted rutabagas and sprinkled with pieces of tasteless bacon. Even the bread was stale!

Her only solace was Sister Alice and two roommates named Marie-Cécile and Salomé. Gisèle suspected Salomé of being Jewish like her but she never dared ask the question. Her father had expressly forbidden her from talking about her faith. Things were different now: she had a new name and she was Catholic. She even had to wear a cross around her neck that her father had given her before entering the convent. "This is your new good luck charm!" he had told her, but she saw the tear rolling down his cheek and knew he was lying. This cross was just a false pretense to make her forget her Jewish origins and shield her from the Nazis.

Despite her unhappiness, Gisèle eventually managed to acclimate to her new life as a Catholic girl abandoned in a totally feminine environment, or rather as she saw it, a women's prison!

Her only escape was reading the few books she had brought with her, including her favorite novel, *Les Misérables*, by Victor Hugo. Cosette's adventures fascinated her. Just like Cosette, Gisèle was locked away in a convent, hidden from the evil Javert who, these days, had developed a German accent. Like Cosette, she saw herself living there for several years until she was an adult and could finally be free. Like Cosette, she might only be a little caterpillar that the Nazis sought to crush, but she knew that one day she would turn into a magnificent butterfly. She would meet her very own Marius, and they would have a beautiful wedding. Unfortunately, she had no Jean Valjean, and she felt terribly alone lying in her little bed every night.

Her parents, and her father in particular, had visited her a few times, but their visits were becoming few and far between. The Mother Superior was extremely cautious and did not want her father to be spotted within the walls of the convent. With his Romanian accent, he seemed entirely too Jewish! This was a military occupation. The militia investigated everything and was quick to denounce any institution suspected of harboring Jewish children.

Alas, this is exactly what happened one day in March 1943. A car full of militiamen pulled up to the entrance of the convent and promptly arrested the Mother Superior. Her second-in-command, in a panic, decided to send all the Jewish girls back home. When Isaac received word, he barely had enough time to pick up Gisèle. Once again, she was going to be taken away from her newly-made friends.

Isaac needed to find another place to hide his daughter and reached out to Marguerite's brother, Georges. He was a thief and a crook but was also very resourceful. He would surely agree to take in Gisèle, in exchange for a few diamonds. Though he lived far away in Tours, Marguerite convinced her brother to come and collect her.

Gisèle met the "black sheep" of the family in April 1943. He was in his forties, handsome, with a meticulously groomed mustache. He was married to a good Catholic woman and had never declared his Jewish status. He was the king of contraband and, despite his hatred for the Germans, he had a knack for the black market and knew exactly how to profit from the occupation.

From Tours, where he resided, he ran a lucrative business selling farm commodities (butter, eggs, chicken, bread) to Parisians. He ensured that the militia and the occupiers would leave him alone by gifting them with some of his finer products. Oh, he wasn't such a bad fellow! He had provided for Jeanne during her short stay at Drancy by sending her a package of eggs, bread and jam. He had even attempted to facilitate her release by bribing the police, but everything had happened too quickly. He hadn't been able to prevent her transfer to Pithiviers and her subsequent deportation to Germany.

Gisèle found herself in the care of her bandit uncle who promised Isaac that he would take good care of her in exchange for a sizeable amount of diamonds.

Unfortunately, Georges had neither the time nor the patience to care for a ten-year-old girl. After only two weeks, he passed her off to his friend, Roger, the coachman for his estate who lived on a farm near Tours. "It's for your own good, little one," he had told Gisèle. "You'll see. Roger is very nice, and you'll be safer in the country. There are no Germans!"

Safer?! Roger was married to the despicable Josette, whose family had been anti-Semitic for generations. She didn't understand why her husband was forcing her to harbor this "Jewish scum". She almost never spoke to Gisèle and confined her to the attic.

Gisèle had learned not to cry anymore; her heart had closed up! She may have had Cosette's story, but she was living it in reverse: she was sent from the convent to the hateful Thénardier household! Like Cosette, she was treated as a small pet that must not make a sound and must obey hand and eye signals. She was required to wash the dishes, clean the floors in the dining room after meals, and care for the horses in the stable. Despite the stink of manure, she felt happiest with the horses. They, at least, understood her and didn't screech at her. She especially loved Bob, a sweet-natured horse with a gray and brown coat. He let her pet him for hours on end and had big dreamy eyes.

Gisèle could have endured this miserable lifestyle until the end of the war if it hadn't been for the most dreadful person in the house: the couple's son, Fernand. She knew deep down that one day he would harm her, just like the men who had taken advantage of Fantine in *Les Misérables*.

So, it's decided! Tonight she is leaving! She closes up her suitcase and sits on the edge of her bed, waiting for the family to go to sleep. Around eleven-thirty, she climbs quietly down the small wooden ladder that connects the second floor to the attic. She scurries noiselessly past Roger and Josette's bedroom, reassured by the loud snoring of the coachman. She makes it downstairs within a few minutes. In the dining room, she carefully opens the front door then closes it gently behind her. She walks cautiously away from the farm and, after a couple yards, begins to run. Free at last! A few hundred yards further she stops, covered in sweat and out of breath, to take a break and lean against the plane tree that borders the main road.

Then the most improbable, incredible, and inexplicable thing happens! She hears the siren go off in the neighboring village. She understands that bombing is about to start. She hides quickly in the ditch bordering the road. After several minutes, she can spot the lights from the canons of the anti-aircraft guns, pointing toward the sky. She hears the growling of the planes getting closer and the crackling of the anti-aircraft cannons. She sees the flashes of the bombs peppering the horizon. She shudders but cannot look away from the Dantesque spectacle that reminds her of the fireworks her parents used to take her to before the war. Finally, the unimaginable happens: the farm that she just ran away from, not thirty minutes ago, explodes before her eyes. A bomb explodes, piercing her eardrums. A bomb has been dropped on Roger, Josette, and Fernand!

Gisèle can't believe it. She is saved! How did the Americans know that she was running away tonight? How did they know that it was time to put an end to Fernand's repulsive behavior? Jean Valjean does exist; and he is a pilot in the U.S. Air Force!

CHAPTER 14
1944
A MIRACLE IN NICE
SISTER ANNE-MARIE

Daniel is incredibly weak having lost twenty kilos in the last few months and today is a mere shadow of himself. He crouches in his cell in the Hotel Excelsior, which has been converted into a prison by the Germans, and waits patiently for death to come. He is resigned. This morning he awoke to the sound of machine gun fire. Something is happening outside! Through his dormer window he spots the German's armored cars going in every direction.

Suddenly, his door is flung open. A German soldier storms in and grabs him. "*Schnell! Schnell!*" he screams, "*Wir müssen gehen*!" He makes Daniel take the stairs four at a time and pushes him toward the large courtyard entrance. The August sun blinds him as he finds himself in the midst of about ten of his fellow prisoners. Two German soldiers guard them menacingly. Someone pushes him violently toward a truck, forcing him to board. This is it then, he thinks to himself. This is the end. He will be shot just like the others. There's no point in resisting. What a shame to die after so many months of suffering, and on such a beautiful summer day! He doesn't even want to live anymore. The last few months have been unbearable; he has been living at the very gates of hell itself.

Yet things had started off so well upon their arrival in Nice in September 1942. Despite his mother's melancholy, Daniel enjoyed wandering the "Promenade des Anglais" with his brother or lolling on the beach. He even had some pleasant encounters along the way; the girls were very pretty and friendly on the Côte d'Azur. But everything took a somber turn starting in September 1943. Isaac sensed the Nazi vise tightening and decided to disband the family for their own safety. Poor little Gisèle was sent to a convent, where she was completely on her own. He and Michel were sent to Don Bosco Catholic School in the center of Nice, not far from their magnificent apartment on the rue de la Buffa. He even had new papers now; his name was Daniel Guilbert, and he had always been a good Catholic.

He didn't stay at Don Bosco for very long. Several weeks after arriving, his ears started bothering him, a fact that might just have saved his life. One day in mid-November, as he lays in his bed in the infirmary, bored to tears and half-dazed by fever and the pain piercing his eardrums, Daniel heard the shrill screams of his classmates – Jews like himself – being carted off by the militia. Those bastards! Soldiers scoured every classroom but, by some miracle, did not come into the infirmary. What had happened to his brother, Michel? He had no idea. The priest who ran Don Bosco was so shaken by the raid that, by the end of the day, he had asked for Daniel to be transferred to St. Roch hospital.

Yet another decision that would save his life! He had scarcely arrived at the hospital when a veritable saint dropped into his life. He became the patient of Sister Anne-Marie, who was immediately taken with the handsome young man whose ears caused him such pain. After several days, she realized that Daniel was suffering from much more than a simple ear infection. His fever remained high and the skin behind his ears had become swollen, red, and painful. Anne-Marie alerted Dr. Lapouze, the chief of service, and together they had made the correct diagnosis: Daniel was suffering from acute mastoiditis. He needed surgery immediately to clear out the pus that had accumulated or he risked sepsis, which would kill him in a matter of days.

Though there were many restrictions on using supplies, even compresses and disinfectants, Dr. Lapouze – also a saint in his own right! – could not bring himself to let this fine young man die. He took Daniel into the operating room and made a deep incision in the swelling behind his ears, doing his utmost to clean out the pockets of pus. All of this was done without anesthetics, of course, apart from a large glass of brandy before the operation. Daniel bit down on a wet cloth to avoid screaming from the pain. By the end of the procedure his eyes rolled back in his head and he fainted.

When he woke, Sister Anne-Marie was at his side, gently dabbing at his brow with a wet sponge. He immediately noticed that the pain in his ears had diminished and thanked heaven for sending these two guardian angels to save his life.

He slowly recovered over the ensuing weeks. The fever dissipated completely by the end of the second week. He was still very weak and his hearing was not fully restored, but he felt much better and enjoyed Sister Anne-Marie's kind attention as she fussed over him. He felt safe in the hospital, far from the militia or the Germans. But he worried incessantly about his brother, Michel. What had happened to him? Had he been rounded up with the other boys or had he somehow escaped? Was there any way to find out? What could Daniel possibly do from his hospital bed?

Sister Anne-Marie had quickly determined that Daniel was Jewish and had decided to protect him. After a month, Daniel was able to stand up and walk and had recovered a large part of his hearing, a miracle in itself considering the severity of his illness and the riskiness of the surgery. But Anne-Marie whispered in Daniel's ear that he should not leave St. Roch Hospital. "It's far too dangerous for you outside! You must actually get sicker so that you can stay here, and I can keep taking care of you." Daniel didn't need convincing. It wouldn't be a stretch to act sicker, particularly considering the sparse rations he was fed each night, usually just a bowl of thin soup. Daniel's cheeks were sallow and he had already lost over forty pounds. He was also happy to stay in Sister Anne-Marie's company. Though his affection for her was strictly platonic, he loved hearing her soft-pitched voice and looking into her almond-shaped eyes.

The masquerade lasted almost three months, thanks to Dr. Lapouze's passive complicity. Daniel might have made it to the end of the war had it not been for the intervention of the very Devil personified – a miserable young female orderly who was transferred to his building in February 1943. Was it pure jealousy at the sight of Sister Anne-Marie conspiring companionably with a handsome young man who was enamored of her? Or was it simply the malice that sometimes inhabits human beings and pushes them to denounce others as a means of wielding their petty power? Whichever the case, the ignorant young orderly with her crass, uncouth manner and nasty scowl had decided that she would no longer put up with Daniel, that smug young Jew who claimed to be so ill.

On March 5, 1943, while Daniel was taking his morning walk in the gardens of the hospital and conversing gaily with Sister Anne-Marie, two imposing black sedans arrived at the hospital entrance. Ten Gestapo agents climbed out and headed upstairs to the first floor. When they came back to the gardens, the treacherous little orderly was guiding them and she was pointing directly at Daniel!

In that instant, he could have escaped. He could have taken off through the streets of Nice and potentially lost the Gestapo. But what was the point? Where would he go? Where were his brother, his sister, and his parents now? Despite Sister Anne-Marie's cries, he did not resist as he was handcuffed and thrown roughly into one of the cars.

The journey to the Hotel Excelsior – transformed into a prison by the Gestapo and the militia – did not take long. He was initially taken to the first floor and violently interrogated. Seated in a chair with his hands tied behind his back and a searing light fixed on him, Daniel encountered pure brutality for the first time in his life. Two militiamen, blinded by their ugly, anti-Semitic hatred, screamed at him for hours on end. One of them pulled out his "Lüger" – a gift bestowed by the German authorities on the most deserving of militiamen – and pressed the gun against Daniel's temple for several interminable minutes. Why did they decide to leave him alone at last? He still didn't know. Perhaps it was because of the desperate subterfuge he had concocted in his panic while being transported from the hospital to the Hotel Excelsior. Because everyone was well aware that he had been operated on for an acute mastoiditis, he simply decided that he would play deaf. So he couldn't answer the idiotic questions put to him by those bloodthirsty dogs! Had they believed him? Maybe not. But they eventually tired of him and, after hours of fruitless interrogation, threw him in a small cell in the attic of the hotel.

A new chapter in his life began then, one that reminded him of the sculpture "*The Gates of Hell*". Daniel often thought of the gruesome image recreated by the brilliant sculptor, Rodin, whom he so loved. Before the war, Daniel frequently went to admire the magnificent sculptures in the gardens of the Rodin Museum, near Les Invalides.

And now he was on death row. His cellmates had names like Bruno Ratti, and Sergio, communists and Jews who he quickly learned served as hostages for the Gestapo, just as he did. One night, Bruno Ratti, who used to sing "O Sole Mio" to Daniel with such passion, was hauled away. He was executed the following day along with ten other "communists" in retaliation for an attack on a German officer's car the previous night.

Yes, indeed. He was at the very gates of hell and had been since the month of March.

Today, as he climbs into a covered truck, most likely to face a firing squad. He is almost relieved. Finally, the gates of hell will open, the night will take him, and his suffering will cease!

But the lucky star that has been protecting him for so long shone on Daniel once more. Just as the truck is about to leave, a car swerves in front of it. It is the French resistance, here to liberate Nice before the allied advance (though he will only discover this later on). They have had enough of the Hotel Excelsior and come to end its murderous activities. A short burst from a machine gun fires and the Germans panic. In a flash, Daniel realizes his moment has come! He leaps from the truck, dodges his way through the pandemonium of the fighting – miraculously avoiding the bullets from both sides that whiz past his head – and hurls himself to safety against the wall of the carriage entrance next to the hotel.

After several long minutes, he peers out and sees no Germans running toward him. They must be far too busy saving their own hides from the fierceness of the resistance fighters, who are utterly determined to root them out completely. Gathering all his strength, Daniel takes off, running at full speed along Durante Avenue, running toward freedom.

Hell has closed its gates, but not on him! He is free at last! Free!

2011
CHAPTER 15
INTERVIEW FOR THE YAD VASHEM MUSEUM

Daniel is visibly tense as he sits beneath the harsh lights. He sits on a couch in his home on the Regavim kibbutz, not far from Caesarea in Israel, with a small microphone pinned to his red sweater. The televised interview is about to start. The journalist, who can be heard but not seen on the screen, calmly explains that this interview will be preserved in the Yad Vashem Archive so that the memories of the survivors of the Holocaust are never extinguished.

It was difficult to persuade Daniel to participate initially, but he understands that, at eighty-five years old, he must now describe what he endured so that the unspeakable never happens again.

The words drift slowly out of Daniel's mouth:

"My father came to France in 1900 from Romania and, in 1925, my parents' marriage was arranged and they were wed…"

Memories return little by little to Daniel's mind.

First comes the memory of his grandmother, Jeanne, who was deported in 1942. Everyone thought that she would surely come home eventually, but after months of waiting at the Lutétia Hotel and hearing the heart-wrenching stories of the survivors, the "living dead"who made it out of the camps, the family resigned itself to the fact that Jeanne would never return. They learned, much later, that she had passed away on the train taking her to Auschwitz in September 1942.

Next, come the memories of his brother and his sister, who were in hiding during the final months of the war. They came back looking haggard and depleted. Michel wasn't able to finish his studies and went to work on an oil rig. Little Gisèle lost all faith in humanity and spent most of her days, in 1945, at the Lutétia Hotel, waiting hypnotically for her beloved grandmother to return. When she wasn't at the hotel, she wandered the streets of Paris; her favorite pastime was riding the bumper cars, which provided her with some distraction.

Marguerite, Daniel's mother, was so overwhelmed with grief that she barely spoke a word. Fortunately, his husband, Isaac, in characteristic fashion, had found the strength to carry on. He returned to his apartment on the rue du Cambodge and found it ransacked and emptied of all furniture. The French government offered him a beautiful Haussmann-style apartment as compensation, but he preferred to restore their little apartment near the Place Gambetta instead. He succeeded in recovering his watch and jewelry shop, "Au Cadran," on the rue Vieille du Temple, where he went back to work. Daniel returned to the shop as well, and worked alongside Isaac until he passed away in the sixties.

Daniel was devastated by the loss of his father, who had been his only source of moral support. Encouraged by Gisèle, he decided to immigrate to Israel. He settled down in the Regavim kibbutz, composed mainly of francophone Sephardic Jews, and learned how to plant avocados, raise chickens, and assemble little plastic toys.

The kibbutz actually saved his life! Here he was part of a caring community and did manual labor. He helped defend this young country that had been at war, yet triumphed, and now offered a permanent asylum for the Jewish people. All of these events gave new meaning to his life after his very existence had been forever shattered by the ordeal at the Hotel Excelsior in Nice. It was at the kibbutz that he met his wife, Léa, a proud and courageous Moroccan Jew, who gave him a daughter named Gali, in 1981.

Gisèle, who had reluctantly returned to school, had the good fortune to meet the man of her life on the "Promenade des Anglais" in Nice in 1953. He was a handsome young man, originally from the north of France, named Albert; she fell madly in love. This miraculous union restored her spirit and led to the birth of her two children, Gilles in 1959 and Isabelle in 1964.

Daniel's brother, Michel, continued his life as a wandering Jew and hardened bachelor. He traveled the world, going from France to Argentina, by way of Israel, where he could always work as a technician on construction sites. The work was hard but it paid well.

The journalist's questions are getting more specific. "When did you witness anti-Semitism for the first time in France? How did you resist the militiamen during your interrogation in the Hotel Excelsior?" Daniel's answers come more or less easily.

After more than two hours, he is glad the interview is over. He is tired, but happy. Now, not only is he a survivor, but he has shared his horrific experience as a legacy for future generations to prevent such a disaster from ever happening again.

EPILOGUE

Saturday, July 21, 2012

The entire family is reunited in a beautiful villa in Caesarea, Israel, on the Mediterranean coast. The weather is splendid and we are about to have a delicious poolside lunch. Everyone is here (or almost). My wife, Isabelle, our two daughters, Sarah and Judith (unfortunately, our eldest, David, had to return to Washington for work), my brother-in-law Gilles, his wife, Cécile, and their daughters, Salomé and Eva. Also present is my father-in-law, Albert—the husband of Gisèle, who passed away in 2001—and an old family friend, Annie. And then there are the heroes of this story: Daniel, 86 years old, accompanied by his wife, Léa, his daughter, his daughter-in-law, and his grandchildren; and Zelma, 87 years old, accompanied by her

children and her cousin, Daniel.

Daniel and Zelma both move slowly; they are stooped and frail. I seat them in the shade, next to the pool, and introduce them for the first time. I tell them about this project and my plans to write this book over the next year. I ask them about a few remaining gaps in the story I'm about to tell. They search their memories and try to answer me as best they can. They notice, for the first time, how similar their stories actually are. They smile at one another, each recognizing a kindred soul.

The pool resonates with the screams of the teenagers rough-housing just across from us. My daughter, Judith, sings "La Vie en Rose," followed by the national anthem of the United States, with perfect American pronunciation. Our family is content.

Daniel and Zelma, thank you for trusting me with your secrets. I hope that you will be proud of these few pages of history that I've transcribed for future generations. I am so honored that my children can claim to be your descendants. Yours is an extraordinary example; you two are living proof that courage, force of will, fearlessness – and just a bit of luck – can surmount even the cruelest of circumstances.

POST SCRIPTUM
WHAT BECAME OF THEM?

People who read the first version of this book, along with giving me wonderful encouragement and sharing in the emotional journey found on these pages, suggested that I shed more light on what became of these characters and how they survived this traumatic period.

And so, dear reader, allow me to share these missing elements with you.

The Holzer-Englander Family:

1- **Renée** was my mother. She died prematurely at age forty-one, but first asked me to write this book. From mid-1943 to mid-1944 she remained hidden in a convent. After the war, she survived this tragedy, as best she could, alongside her older brother, Henri, and her mother, Anna. She managed to focus on her studies and moved back into her apartment on the rue de Saintonge. In 1957, she met my father, Lucien Besnainou, freshly arrived from his home in Tunisia to study medicine. They were married in 1959 and I was born in 1963.

2- **Henri** is my uncle and Renée's brother. After a long career as a general practitioner, he is now retired in Paris. I was able to interview him in 1998 but, since then, he has refused to discuss this period any further. Aside from that first interview, I was able to retrace his story thanks to writings by his wife, Ginette, as well as a book that Father Puech wrote about his own life. Henri had him named "Righteous Among the Nations", the record of which can be found on the following website:
http://www.afmd-allier.com/PBCPPlayer.asp?ID=554407

3- **Anna** was my grandmother. She survived after the war, as best as she could, by working as a seamstress. She passed away in Paris in the early 1990s. I got to know her well. She had a strong German accent and was extremely sweet to me, feeding me her famous "potato latkes", or potato pancakes. She received a small pension, in deutschemarks, from the German government, I think as reparation for the pillaging and theft of the Holzer building in

Mannheim. Unfortunately, she and I never had a chance to discuss the war.

4- **Jacob** was my grandfather. After his arrest in Castelnaudary, he was transferred to Carcassonne prison then Drancy, where he was deported by convoy #68 on February 10, 1944 and gassed in Auschwitz at the age of fifty-one.
5- **Zelma** is my mother's cousin. She survived the war in the southwest of France and got to know my mother well toward the end of the war. She immigrated to Israel in 1947. She still lives in Israel, in Tel Aviv, and has written a short memoir, in German, of she and her husband's experience during the war.
6- **Enieq** was Zelma's husband. A brilliant engineer, he miraculously survived the war in Poland and immigrated immediately afterward to Israel. He passed away a few years back but I knew him well. He spoke very little of those terrible days and I was able to piece his story together thanks to Zelma's book.
7- **Anna's brothers and sisters** are all gone. Here are their stories. I've listed them chronologically, according to age:
    a. **Samuel** and his family were driven into the Bochnia ghetto in Poland, near their home in Krakow. His daughter was forced into prostitution and ended up committing suicide. Samuel tried to join his son, who was in the Resistance, but was arrested and executed.
    b. **Akiva** and his wife were interned in the Plaszow concentration camp in Poland, near their home in Krakow. They both died of dysentery.
    c. **Elsa**, Zelma's mother, immigrated to Israel with her daughter and her husband in 1947. They lived peacefully and happily there until they passed away in the 1980s.
    d. **Regina** was deported from France on convoy #34 on September 18, 1942, and was gassed in Auschwitz at the age of forty. Her daughter, Ruth, handicapped from birth, is believed to have survived and been placed in a Belgian institution after the war. I was never able to find any trace of her.
    e. **Marie** immigrated to Israel after the war and lived out a peaceful existence until she passed away in the 1980s.
    f. **Helene** stayed in France for several years after the war but eventually ended up immigrating to Israel as well. She lived out a tranquil life until passing away in the 1980s.
    g. **Moritz**, who had immigrated to the United States just before the war, lived peacefully there until his death in the early 2000s. I got to know him well, toward his later years,

as I was his only surviving relative in the U.S.; his wife had passed on, and they had no children. With no known living relatives, he was declared a ward of the state of New York and institutionalized as senile. With the help of my uncle Henri, I was able to take him out of that horrible institution and put him in a lovely retirement home in New York City, where he lived out the remainder of his days. I'll never forget how strongly he embraced me when I came to free him from that deathtrap of an institution to which he had previously been committed. He recognized me immediately, even though the judge supervising his guardianship had assured me that he had lost his memory.

h. **Wolf and Hendel Holzer** were expelled from Mannheim by the Nazis in 1939 and sent to Krakow as the Nazis considered them to be Polish. They were savagely gassed in a truck or train wagon.

The Silberman Family:

1- **Gisele** was the mother of my wife, Isabelle. She died of breast cancer in 2001. I knew her very well and was able to interview her extensively in 1998. She had a great zest for life and was extremely proud of her children, who pursued their education even beyond her hopes.

2- **Daniel**, her brother, has lived on the Regavim kibbutz in Israel since the 1960s. We regularly speak over the phone and he had the opportunity to read an early draft of this book. After escaping the Gestapo by the skin of his teeth, thanks to the liberation of Nice by the French Resistance, he succeeded in finding his parents, who were hiding with a friend in Nice. To this day, he still cannot fathom how he was able to survive his internment in the Hotel Excelsior.

3- **Michel**, Gisele's other brother, shut himself up inside the bathroom during the raid of the Don Bosco College. He then escaped and was able to hide out in Nice with a local family until the Liberation. He now lives in Brussels, Belgium. Unfortunately, I was unable to interview him to discuss this period in his life.

4- **Gisele's parents, Isaac and Marguerite**, hid out with friends in Nice until the Liberation. They then returned to Paris, where Isaac was able to get his shop back. Marguerite passed away in the mid-1950s and Isaac in the early 1960s.